NECESSARY ROUGHNESS

New Rules for the Contact Sport of Life

MIMI DONALDSON

NECESSARY ROUGHNESS
New Rules for the Contact Sport of Life

MimiSpeaks! Press All rights reserved.
Published by MimiSpeaks! Press

www.mimidonaldson.com

First Edition

Cover and Interior design: Toolbox Creative, www.ToolboxCreative.com

Library of Congress Cataloguing-in-Publications Data
Library of Congress Control Number: 2010933536
Mimi Donaldson
Necessary Roughness: New Rules for the Contact Sport of Life
ISBN: 978-0-9845724-0-3

2010

DEDICATION

To my mother, whose secret love of the game that she claimed was "too rough," came to light towards the end of her life. I am grateful to her for teaching me never to quit.

And to my dad, the youngest spirit alive, because who could ever speak about Mom without Dad.

Also, to Peyton Manning, who first inspired me to write this book, and coincidentally, shares a birthday with my mother (March 24).

ABOUT THE AUTHOR

"Every time I watch a football game, all I see are the lessons that are rooted in the core of this game: leadership, teamwork, strategy and focus, mentoring, and, above all, courage. All these practical and extremely valuable lessons are in this book."
—Mimi Donaldson

Mimi Donaldson was raised with a comedic view of the world, thanks to early exposure to the fabulous comedy of Carl Reiner and Mel Brooks, Mike Nichols and Elaine May. As children, Mimi and her brother performed comedy sketches around the house. Her brother played the Mel Brooks part in *2,000 Year Old Man;* his Yiddish accent was flawless.

Mom and Dad thought their singing, dancing daughter was destined for greatness. "One day you'll be a star," her mother would tell her, not knowing Mimi would one day entertain people in suits all day long. Mimi's father, a physician, once told her, "What you do is a mixture of mental health and show biz." He was right.

Mimi Donaldson is a motivational speaker who excites, educates and entertains audiences all over the world. She frequently shares the stage with prominent keynote speakers such as Colin Powell, Katie Couric, and Maya Angelou. She has thrilled and inspired over half of the Fortune 100 companies.

Before starting her own consulting business in 1984, she spent 10 years as a Human Resources Trainer at Northrop Aircraft, Rockwell International, and Walt Disney Productions.

She has a B.A in Speech and Communications from the University of Iowa and a Masters Degree in Education from Columbia University. Mimi is co-author of *Negotiating for Dummies,* selling over a million copies, and translated into six languages. Her second book is, *Bless Your Stress: It Means You're Still Alive!* written with C. Leslie Charles.

To talk to Mimi about a presentation for your organization, or to learn more about Mimi and her products, please contact her at:

www.MimiDonaldson.com

mimi@mimidonaldson.com

310.577.0229

ACKNOWLEDGEMENTS

To my sister, Debbie Riley, whose love of "sports movies waaay more then sports" inspires me every day. Thanks, also, for her skillful copy editing.

To my brother, Dr. Ellis Schwied, who was always next to me in my early sports days, and who never misses my birthday/Super Bowl party.

To my brother-in-law, Randy Riley, who has nurtured my love of football for over half my life.

Thanks to my niece, Tanya Schwied, and my nephew, Mark Riley, for your wonderful writing contributions to this book.

Special thanks to Michael LeFevre: your advertising and writing expertise truly "footballized" my book.

Thanks for your contributions:

Dan Moriarty, interviewer extraordinaire, and Lincoln Kennedy, who called me "sweetheart" on air, which made my day.

Jim Tunney, you are the voice of wisdom — thank you.

Rick Telander, bestselling author and sportswriter, who played football for my high school football team. He was Marcie's brother and back then, Marcie was one of my best friends.

Leslie Charles for your invaluable savvy editorial skills, and Suzanna Gagnier for your helpful edits and love of football.

Samantha Holman, my "trusty assistant," who let me work in my pajamas and could read my most illegible scribblings.

Lauren Halperin, who was there at the beginning and helped me get the first words into the computer.

Fields Jackson, Charles Pittman, Mike Pozzi, Gene Stowe, and the staff of a magnificent magazine, *Racing Towards Diversity,* for featuring the first article on my book.

Bonnie Marcus, you are a master interviewer.

Linda Hollander for your brilliance and expertise on sponsorship.

Aggie Kobrin my networking guru, and all my WESTT mastermind women.

And to my cheerleaders, my band of wild, powerful women who root for me always: Sarina Simon, Ronda Ginsberg, Judy Carter, Gina Rubenstein, Dana Ehrlich, Barbara Weiskopf, Eli Davidson, Robyn Holt, Pat Neubacher, Lori Leyden, Farla Binder, Lynne Romanowski, Catherine Girard-Cobb, Barbara Lewis, and Kim Hamer.

CONTENTS

Introduction 1

PART 1: WARM UP • • • • • • • • • • • 7

Chapter 1 9
Starting Lineup: America's Passion

Chapter 2 15
Becoming a Football Girl

Chapter 3 23
How to Watch Football and Eventually Learn
to Love It

PART 2: THE GAME • • • • • • • • • • • 27
Action: Moving the Chains • • • • • • • • 27

Chapter 4 29
The Rules: A Painless Overview

Chapter 5 33
The Draft: The Talent of Recruiting Talent

Chapter 6 41
Lead and Delegate: Trust Every Guy You Line
Up With

Chapter 7 45
Managing Up: Coaching the Coach

Chapter 8 55
Quarterbacking Your Life: Just Say No to
Punting

Chapter 9 59
No Flags: Keep It In Your Pocket

Attitude: A Little Thing Called Character • • • **63**

Chapter 10 65
Commit: Do or Die

Chapter 11 69
Man Up: Or "Welcome to Quebec!"

Chapter 12 73
Stay Light on Your Feet: Reverses,
Scrambling, and Other Broken Plays

Chapter 13 77
Have a Thick Skin: Shut Up and Get Over It

Chapter 14 81
That Little Voice Inside Your Helmet: And It's
Not the Coach

Achievement: The Hall of Fame • • • • • • **85**

Chapter 15 87
The 6 M's: Road Map to Your Hall of Fame

Chapter 16 91
Know Your Mission

Chapter 17 95
Motivate Yourself

Chapter 18 99
Market Yourself

Chapter 19 103
Manage Your Time

Chapter 20 107
Mentor: Have Some and Be One

Chapter 21 111
Measure Your Results

PART 3: THE CLOCK • • • • • • • • • 115

Chapter 22 117
Make the Clock Your Friend (Or at Least
Don't Let It Be Your Enemy!)

Chapter 23 123
Don't Drop the Ball: Time of Possession

Chapter 24 127
Time Out: Blowing Your Internal Whistle

Chapter 25 131
Two Minute Drill: When the Game Is On the Line

PART 4: POST GAME • • • • • • • • • 139

Chapter 26 141
Don't Tell Me a Story: Gimme the Bottom Line

Chapter 27 145
Playing The Gender Game Without a Playbook

Chapter 28 149
The Mute Button and Other Male Fantasies

Chapter 29 155
Hinting: It's Not Romantic

Chapter 30 159
Who's Your Team?

Chapter 31. 163
Zone vs. Man to Man: Shopping vs. Buying

Chapter 32 167
Parting Shot: How Football Saved My Life

INTRODUCTION

"Most people think football is about knocking people down,
but it is really more about lifting people up."
   –Charles Pittman, publisher, Racing Toward Diversity,
   Shurz Communications Inc.

I need to start with a confession. I love football. I'm passionate about the game. But before you write me off as some slobbering fan, let me explain. My journey to football fandom parallels every woman's journey to independence. Through the years, slowly and steadily, women have made a good deal of forward progress in their roles at home and in the workplace. No longer do we feel forced to assume a subservient role or use passive-aggressive behavior to get what we want. We have taken the assertiveness courses of the 1980's and passed with flying colors. Now, we have the confidence to stand up, talk straight, and act with passionate commitment to get what we want.

And that's where football comes in. If you watch football with an open mind, you can learn just about everything there is to know about life: living large, building relationships, cultivating self-discipline and mental hardiness, and most of all persisting and persevering when all seems lost.

The first lesson we learn is that there are times when a certain roughness is necessary, and we mustn't be afraid of confrontation or contact. After all, business is a contact sport. So is life.

Football: the Advanced Course

We've made a lot of progress, but the playing field still isn't level by any means. Nationally, women make 78 cents on the dollar in comparison to men's income. In some states, the figure is even lower. Females represent only 15% of corporate CEOs. Only 17% of our national legislators are women. We have a long way to go.

Football is the advanced course in getting ahead and getting what you want in life and at work. Valuable lesson: do not back off from confrontation. Two teams are eyeball to eyeball on the line of scrimmage. One team's desire is to go *there*. The other team says,

"No you don't." Women have not been comfortable eyeball to eyeball. In the past, I have backed off getting what I want the moment I see the other person is becoming uncomfortable. Not anymore. When I recently negotiated my auto lease purchase, I sent the salesman away four (count them—four) times to get me a lower interest rate. When he started to sweat and look uncomfortable, I flashed on my old habit of backing off. Not this time. I put myself at the line of scrimmage and remained cool and collected and focused on my desire. He wanted to go *that* way to get more money; I wanted to go the other way to pay less. Making him comfortable was *not my job*. Football taught me that, and I got the deal I wanted. I also got an extended warranty, plus four new tires, and since he was sorry the negotiation took so long, he threw in a tank of gas! Sales is a game: the salesman and I are players. My desire to assist other women to play the games of life with courage is what this book is about.

Women and Sports

You don't need to have ever participated in competitive sports to appreciate the lessons in this book. In fact, I never did. In elementary school I would coerce my mother to write me notes to get me out of gym class. "Mom, when I get sweaty, my hair frizzes." Years later I now *pay* a personal trainer to make me sweat.

Women have not always had ready access to participating in sports. In fact, women weren't even allowed to play competitive sports until this century. Thanks to Title IX, young women today have an unprecedented opportunity to engage in sports, and they are doing a magnificent job. We've reached excellence in athletics with true competitive spirit, demonstrating our skill and talent in the pursuit of our dreams. Women showed the world they could compete. And they do it with pride, elegance, strength, and intensity. *Racing Toward Diversity* magazine quotes the Women's Sports Foundation: "It is no accident 80 percent of the female executives at Fortune 500 companies identified themselves as former 'tomboys' — having played sports."

Not for Men Only

Let's get this point right out in the open: there are many women out there who are sick of hearing men extol the virtues of football. When they find out I'm speaking about football, these women come up to me before my speech or training session and say, "I don't like football." My answer is, "Maybe you actually DO like football. You just don't know it yet."

Ask any self-proclaimed "football girl" what she likes about the game. Her answers include commitment, poise under pressure, accuracy, and achieving the impossible. When I began writing this book, my first words were, *"The intention to get to a certain place (on the field or on your career path) makes you unstoppable."* I was watching an NFL football game at the time. The quarterback, Peyton Manning, beat the other team by scoring three times in the last two and a half minutes of the game. He truly was unstoppable.

Manning is talented. Talent alone can account for much success, but not all of it. It takes strategy, commitment, and discipline over time to achieve a level of mastery. Mastery is the ability to enjoy success again and again. Football players are masters at their games. So are we women. Women have never been afraid of hard work. They aren't put off by the long hours of training it takes to compete. They don't shrink from the head-to-head competitive nature of most sports, nor are they strangers to the thrill of victory with all its glory. Women today can fully appreciate the rewards of their dedication to staying in shape and pulling together as a team: family, sports or workplace. We are incredibly good at figuring out what works, and we are amazingly resilient. Women are starting businesses at twice the rate of men these days, and statistics show we are more likely than men to remain in business past the five-year mark. We are women, hear us roar!

> Mastery is the ability to enjoy success again and again.

Why 32 Chapters?

I am a fan of college football, but the NFL has captured my heart. I want NFL talk all the time. Thank goodness for NFL Network on my Direct TV; it sustains me in the offseason. 24/7, 365, aaaahhhh. I am from Chicago, but I do not live and die with the Bears. I have deep love for six teams, and deep hate for four. But all 32 NFL teams have provided me with many tears, laughter, and inspiration over the years. Hence, this book has 32 chapters to honor them all.

Lessons for Us All

Football has taught me to expect more from myself and to see the potential in others. It has taught me patience. Like a quarterback, I have learned to "read" what people intend to do, and let the path in front of me develop and open. I've learned that no one succeeds alone; there are times I've had to wait for my blockers (my team) to help clear the path. I've learned that I have multiple roles. I can be the mentor for younger women like the veterans who mentor the younger football players. I can also learn from the new recruits, the ambitious up and comers as they embark on their careers. Football also helped save my life — literally.

> It's time to get suited up, step on the field and discover the wealth of strategies you've naturally employed, but never connected to football.

The lessons that are rooted in the core of this game, what we can learn, internalize and apply, are too rich and too plentiful to overlook. It's time to get suited up, step on the field, and discover the wealth of strategies you've naturally employed, but never connected to football. The next time you're asked to carry the ball, you'll know exactly what play to call, and why.

Now, no one is suggesting that women should play professional football in the NFL. But never say never. No coach is going to overlook a 6-foot-7, 340-pound female who can run, block, tackle, and also explain why a polo shirt with horizontal stripes doesn't "go" with plaid Bermuda shorts.

PART 1: WARM UP

"Being female has nothing to do with it. I love football. I love teaching. I love these kids."

    –Natalie Randolph, introduced April 9, 2010, as the head football coach at a high school in Washington DC

CHAPTER  1

STARTING LINEUP: AMERICA'S PASSION

"I always turn to the sports pages first, which records people's accomplishments. The front page has nothing but failures."
Chief Justice Earl Warren

Football.

The Ultimate Male Sport.

No bats. No clubs. No rackets. No sticks.

Just big guys in big pads trying to knock down other big guys in big pads. *Mano a mano*, as they say. Eleven guys lined up eyeball to eyeball with the opposing eleven guys. One team is committed to "going there" to the goal. The other team is committed to stopping them from "getting there."

Guys love it. They love playing it. They love watching it.

Brutal. Violent. Physical. Exciting. This is the sport my mother deemed "too rough."

Nobody in my family played contact sports. We played string quartets. But here I am, a self-proclaimed "football girl" and I couldn't be happier about it. Maybe it should come as no surprise that my paying job is cheerleading people to achieve their highest potential. Sometimes I ask myself, how did that happen?

Football: the Best Sport

To me, football is the best of all sports. In my mind there isn't another team sport that matches football for action and strategy. Yes, it's the ultimate male sport, but that doesn't mean we women can't love it too. It requires no bats, no rackets, no clubs and no sticks. Just a ball and a game plan. Some people call it brutal and violent; I call it physical and exciting.

Even though the players are padded and pumped up with adrenalin, on the field the men have permission to be emotional. They not only hit, tackle, run, throw, and catch, they touch, shake hands, high-five, pat, thump, smack, hug, chest bump, choke up, even carry each other off the field. Watching quarterback Brett Favre carrying wide receiver Donald Driver off the field on his shoulders after Driver caught the ball, put a lump in my throat. Without its emotional aspects, football would amount to a track and field event. But when you add in all the elements of planning, sharing, caring, executing and celebrating, you have the perfect game!

In football, you have eleven men pitted against eleven competitors, where baseball is nine against ONE! That hardly seems fair when you stop and think about it. And, baseball is so s-l-o-w. Once in a while there's an exciting moment, but no wonder fans in the stadium have to anesthetize themselves with beer and hot dogs! As George Carlin said, "Baseball has no time limit. We don't know when it's gonna end. We could have extra innings. Football is rigidly timed; it will end even if we have to go to sudden death!" The only thing fast about baseball is the ball. Yawn.

Basketball is five against five. But there isn't a lot of strategy. Yes, there are plays, but they only last a few seconds before the players resort to pure athleticism. It's *too* fast, and the players aren't allowed to touch their opponents. So baseball is too slow. Basketball is too fast. Football is just right.

Football requires planning, strategy, and focus. The coach always has a game plan, and what used to be considered "rah-rah" clichés have become a way of life. Motivation itself has become the new norm, and football is the perfect metaphor. In every game, you see motivational and teambuilding lessons that are crucial in today's hard-fought personal and professional success.

My First Football Lesson

In the introduction I outline the life lessons that football can teach. Well, my first lesson was in the late 70's. My boyfriend was a huge football fan, and he wanted me to watch the games with him so we could spend more time together. I asked him to explain how the game worked. And he did in great detail—during the commercials.

One Sunday afternoon, the whistle blew, the game went to commercial, and Joe caught me wiping a tear.

"What?" he asked.

"Oh, Joe!" I said, "That's my favorite part of football. The guy from one team knocked down a guy from the other team. Then he reached his hand out to help him up."

"What are you talking about?" asked Joe.

"It's just so sweet!" I said.

"Meem," he said, "The whistle blew. The play is over. He's helping the other guy up so they can start knocking each other down again. It's efficiency, not compassion!"

I felt a bit sad, but it was a stunning realization. The whistle blew. The play was over.

When the Whistle Blows

This single example taught me one of the most important lessons of my life, and maybe it will strike you as intensely as it did me. We women have a wonderful capacity to make connections, but we need to learn when to compartmentalize. We need to let go. *When the whistle blows, the play is OVER.* Each moment is a new moment of now. For years, male lawyers have been verbally bashing each other during court proceedings. Afterward, they go to lunch together. Female lawyers tell me they are just beginning to allow themselves that luxury. I'm suggesting that it will serve you to have a short memory, at work as well as at home. Men will appreciate your short memory; it'll make you easier to be a consistent team player.

In the 2009 Super Bowl, the Pittsburgh Steeler receiver dropped a game-winning pass from the quarterback. Instead of sulking or complaining or making excuses, he simply asked his quarterback for another shot, telling him, "Let me get this game for you."

VALUABLE LESSON	
#2	When the whistle blows, the play is OVER.

Neither man was holding onto the previous play. They didn't allow what had just happened to affect the next play. The quarterback did not say, "Well, I don't know. You didn't catch it a second ago." He trusted that the receiver would not make the same mistake. Yes, the next play was a game-winning touchdown reception from quarterback to receiver.

Just as these players did, we need to let ourselves shake off past mistakes and negative circumstances so we can begin the next moment with a clean slate. Football taught me that. It can teach you that, too.

More Benefits

There's more. We women can benefit from the philosophy behind football in all four areas of life: physical, mental, emotional, spiritual.

The extreme physical training and conditioning that football players go through motivated me to start working out and stay in shape. To appreciate the sheer physicality of the game is to understand how satisfying it is to get back into and stay committed to your personal routine of staying strong and fit.

While this book won't cover physical conditioning, it will give you numerous tips to help you nurture your mental, emotional, and spiritual well-being. As I mentioned earlier in this chapter, football involves these aspects, because men have permission to be emotional on the field.

Do sports really matter? Nelson Mandela united a country with a rugby match. He knew that "Sports can awaken hope where there was previously only despair." President Obama said, "When you watch sports, the concerns of everyday life disappear."

Watch a game with these elements in mind, and football will demonstrate examples of how to succeed at work, at home, in your relationships with others, in almost everything you do. This book traces my journey, which parallels the journey of many women, from not being able to tolerate competition to thriving on it. If you approach the tenets of football with an open mind, you may discover countless layers of potential you never knew you had. And it may make Sunday afternoons with your guy a lot more bearable!

> We need to let ourselves shake off past mistakes and negative circumstances so we can begin the next moment with a clean slate.

CHAPTER  2

BECOMING A FOOTBALL GIRL

"Surround yourself only with people who are going to lift you higher."
—Oprah Winfrey

No Contact Sports for Us

I was born into a family where we pursued the intellectual, not the physical. We didn't play contact sports; we played string quartets. The only competition in our household was watching contestants vie with each other in TV game shows such as *To Tell the Truth*. Could anyone in our family guess the right answer before one of the panelists on the show did? You're thinking "riveting," right? Well, we enjoyed the mental challenge.

For a girl who turned out to be such a sports nut, I didn't start out that way at all. No Chicago Bears for us; no Sundays or holidays hunched in front of the tube. My brother remembers the only trip to Soldier Field we ever made was to see the fireworks display on the Fourth of July.

My earliest genuine sports memory was watching boxing with my beloved grandfather. Of course, he called it "The Fights." I was about seven years old at the time and my brother was five. We would go to Grandma and Grandpa's house on Fridays to spend the night so our parents could have a date night. There I was, sitting on Grandpa's knee, hiding my eyes because the men on the screen were punching and slugging it out. They seemed to be hurting each other, and I couldn't figure out how or why anyone would consider watching this kind of thing fun. My brother didn't seem at all bothered by the violent exchange of blows, but I hated it. But I loved my Grandpa! Even after my dear Grandpa tried to allay my fears by telling me it was just a sport and they weren't really hurting each other, I still didn't like it. It was too brutal. Too violent. Too real.

Fortunately, my most lasting memory of those Friday nights was eating saltine crackers slathered with raspberry preserves. I loved it when those tiny seeds would get stuck in between my teeth. This delicacy remained one of my favorite snacks for the first 12 years of my life. Yum.

The Baseball Period

My journey into spectator sports actually began with all those hours of watching the Friday night fights, and the next step was baseball. My dad introduced us to America's favorite pastime. Baseball was my family's only spectator sport. In Chicago parlance, Mom was a Northsider, so she was a Cubs fan. The hospital where dad worked (he was a doctor) was on the South Side, so he considered himself a White Sox guy.

So we were either at a Cubs game or a White Sox game. We rooted for both! You may ask, "How could you?" My answer is, "Our family played string quartets. We didn't know from competition; what was important was every player (in our quartet) ends at the same time."

It was about this time that I gained another notch on my sports belt. There we were at the baseball game, my dad, brother (8 years old) and me (10 years old). It was the bottom of the ninth inning and one of the teams was down by two points. There were two outs, and two men on base — batter up!

My father shook his head slowly as he said in a rather ominous tone, "He's gonna be a hero or a bum." It sounded really scary to me, and I remember feeling bad for the guy with all that pressure on his shoulders. My little brother screamed, "Yeah!" enthusiastically, like he couldn't wait to see the gore or the glory. He loved the either/or of these situations, the absolute goodness or badness of the outcome. He was really into the "win or lose" nature of the game.

I hated it. I would have rooted for the poor batter even if he were on the other team, any team. And I probably did. I couldn't stand the thought of anyone being a bum or a loser. In my heart I wanted everybody to be happy. I wanted a win-win. As you can see, as a sports fan I obviously still had a long way to go.

The Bumper Pool Period

But life went on and organized sports went in and out of my consciousness. During my teen years we had a bumper pool table in the family room. I was in high school by this time, and I loved playing the game. I got really good at bumper pool, playing every day after school, and was very proud of myself. One day as I cued up for a shot, I felt a presence nearby. I looked up and sure enough, Mom was watching from the stairs. She was shaking her head slowly from side to side, and her face didn't look very happy. After the boys left, I asked Mom what was wrong and she said these fateful words, "Miriam (my serious name), you must stop beating the boys. If you keep beating the boys and winning, they won't like you."

My eyes filled with tears. It was the first piece of bad advice my Mother had ever given me. I struggled to understand. "But, Mom," I whimpered, "I'm good. If I'm better than they are, I have to beat them. Do you think I should let them win, like Dad used to let us win at Checkers when we were little?" I don't remember what she said after that. I realize now I took her cautionary words at face value, especially the part about the boys not liking me if I beat them.

I was being told not to compete, not to strive to win, but to throw the game for the sake of social acceptance. Women of my mother's generation got what they wanted from their husbands not by standing up as equals but by using passive-aggressive behavior. Women of my generation (even as teens) rebelled against that practice, espousing the "equal partner" theory instead of the end-around strategies our mothers embraced.

> Women of my mother's generation got what they wanted from their husbands not by standing up as equals but by using passive-aggressive behavior. Women of my generation (even as teens) rebelled against that practice, espousing the "equal partner" theory instead of the end-around strategies our mothers embraced.

A few years later, when my mom was stumping for the passage of the ERA (Equal Rights Amendment) in Illinois, I reminded her of the advice she had given me about not beating boys at bumper pool (or any other competitive pursuits). "Miriam," she declared in her crisp feminist tone, "I would never say anything like that." She had completely blocked that moment out of her mind! I dropped the subject, but some years later I was once again reminded of that moment.

Getting in the Game

I went to work as a Human Resources trainer. One day the male and female trainers were comparing salaries. I realized that the men were being paid more than the women even though we held more advanced degrees and had more experience than our male peers. Mom's words came immediately back to me.

I thought, "If I want that big house on the beach and a fancy car to drive and the latest fashions to wear, I'd better start beating some of the boys." A few of my girlfriends coyly suggested that I just marry one of them, but beating them seemed a whole lot easier at the time, and more fun.

In 1982, the movie, *Diner,* came out. Having fully embraced football by then, I loved the part in the movie where Eddie gives his fiancée Elyse a football quiz of 140 questions, with Eddie asking the questions. If she passes, they get married. Otherwise, "if she fails the test, it's out of my hands," Eddie says. I almost wish someone could have given me a football trivia test. I would've kicked some serious butt.

It didn't take long for me to realize that all you have to do is go to a sports bar during a game, sit on a stool and sip a drink, and men will give you a quiz. (See CHAPTER 30: "Who's Your Team?")

Around this time I decided to "get in the game" by getting physical and I came up with my first real participatory sports challenge. In 1983, I trained for my first and only marathon. Just one year later, I started my own business. Was this a coincidence? I think not! Here's how I see the two as being related. Training for a marathon requires vision, determination, and a plan. You don't just skip out of the house and run 26.2 miles without any preparation.

Starting my own business was my version of taking a risk and not playing it safe anymore. No more bi-monthly salary checks from Daddy Disney or Papa Northrop (my past employers); I was now totally and completely on my own. Like running a marathon, starting your own business requires vision, determination and a plan. You don't just walk away from a steady job without any preparation. Becoming an avid football fan helped motivate me to develop the skills it took to break away from the crowd and run my marathon. And completing the marathon gave me the courage to break away from my everyday job and go out on my own.

It's no surprise to me that after running a marathon I decided to start running my own business. The word itself is significant. "Running" is what football players do. And "running" their business is what entrepreneurs do! How's that for a perfect parallel?

Running my own business and competing with other speakers for client engagements was now my version of a contact sport. Speaking in front of thousands of people was my version of Sunday afternoon on the field, without pads and without a helmet.

My boyfriend at this time was a 49ers fan from Northern California. We enjoyed many games on the couch as well as in the stands. It was in Candlestick Park during this period that I fell in love with the back of Jerry Rice's thighs. (See next chapter: "How to Watch")

While I started out watching sports with others, I now love watching football by myself. When the phone rings on Sundays, I answer, "Happy Football Sunday," and I only answer during commercials. I try to live by the credo "friends and family over football—except during playoffs." There's a limit to my devotion.

And here's a lovely piece I have to add so you get the full extent of my love for the game and its significance to me. Since 1988 when the NFL moved the date of the Super Bowl to early February (instead of mid

January), every seven years, the Super Bowl happens on my birthday, February 4th . So, every year I get to celebrate my birthday as a football girl. My family participates in a combo Super Bowl/Mimi's birthday season party, complete with chicken wings, popcorn, chips and salsa during the first half, with birthday cake and singing at half time. My dear family indulges me.

And if you ever run into me at a sports bar, I'm not playing the part of Elyse in *Diner*. I've taken on the role of Eddie. I'm the one asking the questions!

CHAPTER 3

HOW TO WATCH FOOTBALL AND EVENTUALLY LEARN TO LOVE IT

"I like sports movies waaay more than sports."
–sister, Debbie Riley

First off, it doesn't hurt if you like the company of men. Yes, men are different from women and most of the time we can be thankful for that. They can be a little rough around the edges, but you have to love their appreciation of the thrill of a contest, especially when there's a group of them around a TV and a game is on.

Step One: Watching the Spandex

Get over your past judgments and simply observe what's happening on the playing field. Admire the physical prowess of the athletes on both sides. Appreciate their splendid bodies and sheer athleticism. They are strong and capable. Any one of those players could carry you and me across a flooded street so we don't get our feet wet.

VALUABLE LESSON	
#3	Spend a little time getting into the shape they've gotten themselves into!

I hope you appreciate the image. These guys spend a lot of time working out and getting into shape. So spend a little time getting *into* the shape they've gotten themselves into!

And if I may be so bold, please allow me to point out my favorite part of the male anatomy: that wonderful hunk of muscle that runs up the back of a well-developed thigh. Visualize that one spot. How can you not love it? If that image doesn't get your blood moving a little faster, grab a small mirror and exhale. I hope you find a little bit of fog on its surface.

For me, isolating and looking at that single spot on a well-tuned athlete is like watching a thoroughbred on the racetrack. Hey, what's not to enjoy about watching 22 men at the peak of their physical prowess running around a field in helmets, pads and spandex—they're the only ones who can wear that dreaded fabric and pull it off! Hey, the eye candy is there for your enjoyment; see and savor along with me.

Step Two: Root for Dramatic Plays

Ratchet up your enthusiasm (relax, it's good for you). Root for dramatic plays, regardless of which teams are playing or who is winning. Appreciate and applaud the moves, the strategy, the overall engagement of the players, whoever they are. I'm talking about the kinds of plays that cause fans to get up out of their seats without even knowing they've done it.

Here are a few easy-to-identify plays that get a crowd going (and I suggest you go along with it):

- A wide receiver stretching out for an impossible catch, almost parallel to the ground, defying gravity, almost FLYING. It's practically a form of ballet in all its primitive beauty. And you always know when a great play (or an almost great play) has taken place because they show the instant replay over and over in slow motion... sigh... The repetition is a clue.

- A running back with three 300-pound linemen hanging on to his waist, his legs, any piece of him they can get hold of, trying to drag him down, while his feet keep moving, as he pushes, strains, and gets an extra few yards for his efforts. For me, watching this kind of effort is the game at its most magnificent and it comes with its own obvious life lesson: determination and force of will to reach a certain place can make you unstoppable.

- A quarterback dropping back to pass, as a wall of attackers comes toward him. He then scrambles out of their grasp to complete an unrehearsed pass to an alternate receiver (not the target he intended because of the rush). Any quarterback who can scramble like this numerous times per game and pull it off is headed for the Football Hall of Fame.

Once you've mastered the art of appreciating great plays, it's time for the ultimate mark of a true fan.

Step Three: Pick Your Team

When it comes to picking teams, there are all kinds of reasons for making the choice. Perhaps you like the colors of the uniform or the team logo. Maybe you have geographic loyalty, such as the home team where you grew up or where you live now. If you don't have a favorite team, my suggestion is to start watching the quarterbacks in the game. Research their team and head coach. Or, if you share my passion, go for a wide receiver with those killer thighs. That should keep you occupied for a while. Keep track of how your chosen player or players do throughout the season.

Check the sports section in your newspaper or the sports headlines on the web or on the TV sports news to keep up. If you're single, this is a great thing to do in a coffee shop or Internet café. You might just attract another fan, you never know. Don't worry about sports overload.

Your team will play only one game per week, and there are just 16 games per team in the regular season. Once you pick your favorite team and favorite players, you can muster enough interest to keep you going for a season. And if your interest begins to flag, you've always got those great thighs or trim waists or magnificent forearms to hold your attention.

Perceive it as a Drama

Another way to get into football is to perceive it as a drama. Use my sister Debbie's approach and pretend you're watching a sports movie. I'm convinced this is how men look at football games, although they'd never admit it. What they like about the sport parallels what attracts a lot of women to soap operas.

In your typical soap, a character you've watched for several years can get unceremoniously killed off. "Eek!" you may say in a state of shock. "What happened to my Tony?" And he stays killed off. Or does he? Sometimes, Tony wasn't killed off at all, and he comes back. How dramatic is that? Sometimes life (and death on TV) can be so unpredictable.

Well, it's the same with football. You want drama? Just tune in to the game and keep your eyes peeled!

PART 2: THE GAME
ACTION: MOVING THE CHAINS

"Football teaches you that life is hard, but it can be immensely rewarding. Even thrilling. Joseph Conrad said we live as we dream, alone. And that is true. But sometimes we come together in teams. Which is another football gift."

–Rick Telander, sportswriter, and bestselling author, from his book, Like a Rose.

CHAPTER 4

THE RULES: A PAINLESS OVERVIEW

"If winning isn't everything, why do they keep score?"

–Vince Lombardi

The Basics

Now let's settle in for some of the basic information on football in America, just in case you need some of the nitty gritty about the game and the NFL (National Football League). If you already know the essentials of my favorite sport, either consider this a refresher course or feel free to skip this part and catch up with me at the end of the chapter.

In a football game, there are two teams, the offensive team (they have the ball) and the defensive team (they want the ball). Each side has 11 players. Here's an interesting point: if a team has more than eleven players on the field, it gets penalized. If a team has fewer than 11 players, it doesn't matter. I guess you could say that if a team can succeed with fewer than 11 players on the field, it rocks (but this doesn't happen often).

The object of the game is to score points by moving the ball to the opposing team's end zone. The two major ways of scoring are the touchdown and the field goal. A touchdown is when a player gets into the end zone via running with the ball or catching a pass once inside the end zone. This is worth 6 points. A field goal is a when a team is close to the end zone, but hasn't reached it, so a specialty player kicks the ball through the goal posts (or at least tries). This field goal is worth 3 points if the kick is successful.

A football game consists of a series of "downs." A down is a short individual play that makes up the structure of the game. In between each play, the ball is dead, which means that one can't just pick it up and start running. Each play starts at the line of scrimmage, the spot where the dead ball is. The offensive team (the one with the ball) has to go at least ten yards within four downs. The yards are marked on the sideline with chains. If they don't go the full ten yards (which means the defensive team did their job), the defending side now gets the ball and has to do the same. Usually when an offensive team hasn't gone 10 yards in three plays, they use the fourth down to punt the ball to the opposing team, forcing that team back into their own territory as far as possible from the defending goal line.

In between plays, coaches take players out and put other players in. This happens in the time the teams are allowed between almost every play. Sometimes one player gets substituted, but on other occasions (when things are really going wrong) it could be the whole team (or lineup) that changes. It all depends on the situation.

The Clock

The game is divided into 4 quarters, each lasting 15 minutes by the official game clock. This may sound as if the game will be over in an hour, but the official clock, like a local subway route, makes a lot of stops. At the end of 60 minutes of (official) play, the team with the most points wins. If the score is tied, the game goes on (it's called overtime) until one of the teams scores. And unlike hourly employees, the players don't get extra pay for overtime (hey, they already make enough money to show up and suit up!).

So now you know why football games last so long. That official game clock stops after every play. When there's an incomplete pass (the player misses the ball or drops it), the clock stops. Whenever a ball carrier runs out of bounds, the clock stops. As if that's not enough stoppage, each team has 3 timeouts per half. So, the clock stops a lot. This often frustrates newbies, but go with it. Truth be told, this is one of the aspects of the game that makes football great. I'll give you more inside scoop about the clock later.

When a player is running with the ball (whether it was handed off to him by the quarterback or he's caught a pass) the player is considered "down" (or stopped) when any body part other than his hands or feet touch the ground. When an opponent makes this happen, it's called a tackle. If it happens by accident (a slip on wet grass for example) without an opposing player touching the ball carrier, the ball carrier can get up and continue running. Runners are also considered "down" when they run out of bounds or are pushed out of bounds.

Each play or down begins with a snap, where the guy in the middle of the offensive line (the Center) passes the ball through his legs to the hands of the quarterback behind him. Each play is over when the ball becomes dead as the result of a tackle or missed pass. The ball is placed or spotted where it last became dead. If the play was a dropped pass or incomplete pass, the ball comes back to the original line of scrimmage, and the team is charged with one of those four downs, they are allotted in their attempt to score.

The simple math of the game dictates that if your team can keep getting 10 yards every three plays, they'll eventually score. They'd have to. The field is only 100 yards long. But it's obviously not that easy. Hence, the inventive strategies they use (X's and O's.) But we are not going to get into all that.

You are the Offense

Now, throughout this book, we will mostly concentrate on the Offense. That's because YOU are the Offense. You have the ball. You're the one with a goal to achieve, whether it be in business or love or life in general.

Not that defense isn't important. A common phrase is, "Defense wins championships." True, it gets the ball back to the offense. What wins games, though, is the offense scoring points: getting touchdowns and kicking field goals.

In football, the defense can score points when interceptions and fumble recoveries result in a defensive score. If your team's defense can get a few points every game, you're probably headed for the playoffs.

In case you're wondering what all of these rules about football have to do with you, here's the point. When you carry the ball in your own

> When you carry the ball in your own life, you score points too, in your career and at home.

life, you score points too, in your career and at home. For your purposes, consider your life has a game clock. Sometimes, whether you're in an offensive or defensive position, you have to stop or call a time out. You need to check your game plan and how it's worked for you so far so you can regroup. Always keep the big picture in mind (the goal, how to score) and most of all, be patient.

CHAPTER  5

THE DRAFT: THE TALENT OF RECRUITING TALENT

"Sure, luck means a lot in football.
Not having a good quarterback is bad luck."

–Don Shula

Whether you're looking to be chosen or you're the one doing the choosing, there's a talent to recruiting talent. In football, several months before the season starts, before a team suits up, before the first kickoff is booted, there is an event called the NFL Draft. Like the first robin in the spring, the draft signals the beginning of each season, long before the first game in September.

The Draft is a closely watched, much celebrated ritual by diehard fans, as new players enter professional football from college. The purpose of the Draft is to ensure all teams have the ability to choose from the same highly talented athletic pool, allowing for the teams to be more evenly matched and potentially equally competitive. Coaches look for new players with certain strengths and skill sets to balance out any weak positions. For example, a coach won't draft a running back if the team is short on tackles. They look for, screen, and hire needed players just as a company does.

Be Shrewd

In football, just as in business, there is a very real need to be shrewd about how dollars get spent. Of course, in professional football, contracts can climb into the tens of millions of dollars. While your profession might not command that kind of money, you want to be every bit as selective as a coach in hiring your work team, so you can find the right person for the right job. Scouts and coaches spend endless hours collecting and analyzing data, watching game footage of college students, talking to agents, managers, other coaches, parents, and even players' spouses. Every exhaustive form of evaluation is helpful.

VALUABLE LESSON	
#4	In football, just as in business, there is a very real need to be shrewd about how dollars get spent.

Oddly, the best players in the league, the players who last a long time (which in football is 10 years or so), aren't always the guys who were picked highest in the Draft. More often than anyone wishes, the high picks turn out to be duds (go figure!). And to finish this peculiar anomaly, the guys who get drafted near the bottom often end up being the game's keystone players. In addition, just because a player comes from a big NCAA college football program doesn't mean he'll turn out any better than a guy from some school out in the boonies that no one's ever heard of.

VALUABLE LESSON	
#5	While your profession might not command that kind of money, you want to be every bit as selective as a coach in hiring your work team, so you can find the right person for the right job.

A team's roster is pretty fluid, which is why the Draft is so important. Every season a number of players retire or get cut, and every season a number of new players come into the game. The Draft, with its infinitely complex structure, determines which teams get which new players. But it can be broken down into some basic universal principles. In looking at the process of evaluating talent, three key components emerge.

The Three C's

For simplicity's sake, let's call them The Three C's: Capabilities, Character, and Chemistry.

- Capabilities are simply a new recruit's credentials (education, experience, and accomplishments). Each player's skills and performance record are taken into account. The recruit's education and related work experience are also taken into account. As you've probably already surmised, capabilities are the most measurable of the three C's.

- Character is more intangible, of course, and it covers two main areas: the player's behavior on the field and off. Bad behavior on the field (or in our jobs) is pretty easy to see and easy to correct. Bad behavior off the field is tricky, but can have a huge effect on the rest of the team and the possible success or failure of the entire franchise. Even if you live in a cave, you've seen headlines censuring professional athletes who thought they could get away with all kinds of social transgressions. Even the best player in the world can lose his fan base if the offense is extreme enough. In the business world, think of Enron and the Wall Street meltdown (as you know, I could go on and on).

- Chemistry is about fit. How does a potential team member's skills fit with the needs of the team? Will the player's personality and style blend in with the coach and other members of the team? Once in a while there's a loner who seems to go his own way. This doesn't automatically mean he's a bad choice, but it does mean that the coaching staff (and maybe a few key players) will have to put forth extra effort so they can help this player realize his potential. Perhaps this reminds you of work teams you've been a part of. Some people are a better fit than others, and some teams gel better than others.

The First C: Capabilities

In the NFL, the Draft is the main method for assessing capabilities and credentials. You could think of it as an annual six-day job fair

VALUABLE LESSON	
#6	Recruiting the right people for the team is vital!

for prospective players. Every spring more than 300 players go through a series of drills, tests, and interviews with over 600 NFL scouts, head coaches and their assistants, general managers, and team owners. The players complete drills such as running the 40-yard dash, bench pressing weights, doing vertical and broad jumps, the three-cone drill, and the 20-yard shuttle (where a player runs from sideline to sideline as fast as possible, demonstrating lateral mobility), in addition to other physical tests.

While all of this hoopla is going on, some colleges sponsor Pro Days, inviting NFL decision makers to have an up-close-and-personal look at prospective candidates.

Seems like a lot of trouble, just to find a few guys who can run or pass or knock down other guys, doesn't it? Maybe. But it's obviously worth it, or they wouldn't do it. There's a lot of importance placed on the Draft, and therein lies an important lesson for us—recruiting the right people for the team is vital!

If you're in a position to select new hires, you might ask yourself, what would it take to approximate the NFL Draft practice for recruiting the best candidates for job openings in your organization? In what ways could the candidate's capabilities be tested, measured, or verified? What series of job-related exercises equivalent to jumping, dashing, and shuttling could you put them through to have a better sense of how they might fit? How about testing their computer skills or having them conduct sample marketing calls during your interview? Maybe you could conduct group interviews so existing team members have the opportunity to give potential recruits the once-over.

> **VALUABLE LESSON**
>
> **#7** If you're in a position to select new hires, you might ask yourself, what would it take to approximate the NFL Draft practice for recruiting the best candidates for job openings in your organization?

Considering that players who seem to be the top Draft picks don't always work out as expected, be careful about getting blindsided by the qualifications of what appears to be an exceptionally talented candidate. A coach or general manager can easily be impressed with the lightning speed of the candidate with the fastest time in the 40-yard dash. But how will that player perform in all the other aspects of the game including when he's off the field?

The Second C: Character

Now we revisit Character, the ultimate intangible. Character includes a recruit's history on other teams, a record of past transgressions or awards, indicators of poor judgment or a squeaky clean record. Throughout the process of The Draft, recruiters pay close attention to the balancing act between a player testing positive for marijuana use versus having superior skills on the field. Typically in football, high-level skills win out. Why? Coaches and owners tend to risk historical misconduct, confident that any bad behavior won't carry over into a player's professional life.

They also put much stock into their own ability to keep a tight rein on a player off the field, often having turned around several players over the course of their coaching careers. Instilling character remains an important part of professional sports, even though it doesn't always appear that way. There are many more unreported successes in this regard than the tabloid headlines lead you to believe.

It might be best NOT to follow the typical NFL practice on this one. It's critical for you to contact numerous sources who can vouch for a candidate (or not), and do extensive checking on a candidate's referrals. In any workplace, employers simply cannot risk having their team members repeating past indiscretions or displaying poor judgment. Unlike professional football, when selecting a new hire, the character should already be well established. You have enough to do in your job without adding character building to your job description!

The Last C: Chemistry

The last "C," Chemistry, means having the right fit of skills and personality to meld with current team members. Football managers and coaches constantly keep this in mind throughout the entire recruiting process. And employers need to as well. Hiring the best talent doesn't necessarily translate into the most wins; if the team needs a big burly defensive lineman, the coach may not want to draft a new speedy running back. Make

> Hiring the best talent doesn't necessarily translate into the most wins.

sure your latest "find" not only complements existing players in your department, but also fills a gap. Finding the right candidate may require more than one interview. You may need to closely observe your interviewees and meet with them more than once to gauge how they interact with others and what their tendencies might be. This extra effort usually pays off. In football it makes things better for the players, better for the coaches, and better for the team. Why would you want to settle for anything less with your team?

One More: Passion

Along with The Three "C's," there's a fourth component I want to throw in. I couldn't find a synonym that started with a "C" but it's really important and it doesn't require a lot of preparation. However, in my mind, it's the most crucial requirement.

Make sure your candidate has PASSION; make sure this person absolutely LOVES playing the game.

Over the course of any interview, always be sure to find out how passionately the candidate feels about the job at hand and about the mission of your organization. Passion is a significant element in the success of your team. It keeps the fires burning when things fall apart. It keeps the players getting back up after they've

> Passion is a significant element in the success of your team.

failed or been knocked down. Passion is something you can't force on another person. It has to be there, deep inside. It makes all the difference in the world. Any coach will tell you that.

The NFL has a big advantage, and I think you'll appreciate it. If a player isn't working out for you and your team, you can always trade him. That's not quite so easy for you, and that's why you want to make the best possible choice the first time around.

CHAPTER  6

LEAD AND DELEGATE: TRUST EVERY GUY YOU LINE UP WITH

"Be bold, and mighty forces will come to your aid."
–Basil King

Being in charge is a big job but it can also be a joy. It is the rare person who goes through life without ever needing to ask other people to produce some kind of result. How do you get results from others, whether they are family, co-workers, employees, or committee members? Just as the football coach guides and encourages the quarterback to pass the ball off to his teammates, we all need a lot of practice in passing the ball (or in our terms, delegating). It sounds simple, but it isn't always easy.

The Soccer Mom

For example, Friday night Janice is on her way home from work. She should be looking forward to the weekend but she's not. Instead she's dreading the next morning's soccer game.

Janice is in charge of the "Snack Packs" for her twins' soccer team. In the beginning of the season, she carefully typed up and distributed schedules so each parent would know when it was their turn to bring juice boxes and orange sections. Most people have followed through, and snack time has gone well.

But tomorrow is Alison's turn. Alison, also known as, "Oh, no! Not Alison! Anyone but her!" is notorious for dropping the ball. The last time it was her turn she "forgot." To make matters worse, she and her husband had a screaming fight on the sidelines over which one of them would have to leave the game to hit the store and buy snacks. Meanwhile, imagine how well the game is going for an entire team suffering from near starvation and crankiness (and their frustrated parents on the sidelines).

Janice is nervous, imagining tomorrow's game. Should she stop and get some backup snacks just in case? She briefly wonders if she could simply call in sick. Should she tell her husband to go without her? After all, it's not her job. Or is it?

Let Them Succeed or Fail

Here's a football insight to help you handle your delicate situation. On the field, having a short memory is the standard. Once a player has been given the ball, he is trusted by his teammates, no matter what his history has been. Maybe he fumbled on the last play, or had a flag thrown because he broke the rules. Whatever he did is now considered history. Football is very much "in the moment."

Every coach knows that true leadership often involves allowing your players the chance to succeed—or fail. It's a victory when it works, a harsh lesson when it doesn't. But how are you going to discover the potential of every member on your team if you don't give each individual a chance to show their mettle?

Have a Backup

There's another football secret Janice needs to know about. It's called having a backup. In football, there are actually 53 players on a team but only eleven men are on the field at any given time. Most positions have at least one back up player who can step in and share the duties of the first in case of injury or other circumstances. When a running back gets smashed by three 270-pound linemen, he comes out of the game for at least one play to rest and recoup. Another running back takes his place.

VALUABLE LESSON	
#8	You don't make a big deal out of the mistakes; you save that energy to celebrate the successes.

In Janice's case, she could stash some snacks in the trunk of her car the day Alison is in charge. In case Alison drops the ball, Janice can quietly step up to the social line of scrimmage where she ends up being a hero without making a big fuss about Alison's *faux pas*.

Pure and simple, it's called teamwork. As in football, you don't make a big deal out of the mistakes; you save that energy to celebrate the successes. Yes, it's nice to have a backup and sometimes you need to be the backup. Some rise to the occasion; others fumble. The mistakes get covered as well as possible and then you're on to the next play. It is pure power to know what your job is, choose to have a short memory, and stay focused on the present!

CHAPTER 7

MANAGING UP: COACHING THE COACH

"The coach should be the absolute boss, but he still should maintain an open mind."
–Red Auerbach, NBA coach.

In the corporate world, a lot of people are under the impression that management works in a one-way flow from the top down. Considering the memos and orders that come from the top, it may seem that way but actually, it's not. Ideally, communication within an organization flows both ways, down and up. There's a problem though. Many employees don't know how to manage their bosses, or worse, they don't think they can—or should.

In football, the structure of a team is similar to that of a corporation. It's the two-way communication flow that engenders a team's success. Even though the majority of information comes from the coach down to the players, smart players know how to coach their coach.

Boss: Not a Four-Letter Word

It helps to keep in mind coaches (and corporate managers) are people, too. Star defensive player, Lincoln Kennedy, says coaches really

earn their money. Kennedy says this about coaches: "They are 'social workers.' They have to manage the team and keep the peace. And they don't have the power to release a player; that has to come from upstairs. The player is worth millions and the coach's job is to figure out a way to work with him." Sound familiar? Like good coaches, top managers have to find ways to work with the "star performers" in their departments, no matter how obnoxious those employees may be!

While coaches don't like back talk from players, they do appreciate feedback. There's a big difference between the two! A player that comes to his coach with ideas and suggestions is a player on his way to becoming a team leader. To coach the coach, the player explains what he needs, what he thinks will work, and offers solutions. Imagine how receptive the coach will be to feedback of this quality. This is the difference between complaining and problem solving and it works.

> Coaches (and corpo-
> rate managers)
> are people, too.

Head coaches, assistant coaches, and squad coaches all value the player who can describe a particular problem he's facing. The player might even offer his own solution, an alternative to the pattern he's supposed to run or the route he's assigned. When the coaching staff has an open-door policy and encourages the two-way flow model, a team will almost always benefit. It's true for us, too.

The "Ain't It Awful" Game

It's a common tendency for employees to feel they're being victimized, either by the boss or by the company for which they work. When people play victim, they relieve themselves of having to be responsible for their behavior. They let themselves pretend that these things happen to them and they have no choice. They turn into Prima Donnas. Sports shows are full of stories about these kinds of players. Of course, the "things that happen to a person" are usually "unfair" or "unreasonable." And they're not responsible. These individuals feel they have no say in the matter. As you can imagine, the situation quickly becomes a downward spiral.

Being a victim is a passive undertaking but it also has an aggressive component. It first requires the victim to abdicate all responsibility and assume a "do nothing" attitude until the victim gets bored enough or ticked off enough to finally blow up. Victims travel in flocks. They find each other and compare notes on the injustices done to them. They try to outdo each other with their tales of woe.

> When people play victim, they relieve themselves of having to be responsible for their behavior.

When I taught school, I learned a victim game called "Ain't It Awful." It was often played in the teacher's lounge. It went something like this: Mr. Willard would say, "You think *you* have it bad? I have David in my class this year!" Then there'd be a chorus of sympathetic "Oooo's!" and clicking of tongues. Then Ms. Meyer would say, "David's a problem, all right. But I have Howie *and* his twin brother!" More and bigger "Oooo's!" Ms. Meyer wins. She received the loudest, longest, most sympathetic response. She won because she had it worse than anyone else. In "Ain't It Awful," the biggest victim always wins. Employees do that and so do many other people. They play "Ain't It Awful," but they walk away feeling worse than when the game started. The victimizing vents a little steam but it's negative thinking. The downward spiral gets reinforced and that's what makes it destructive. You know what I mean if you've ever been stuck in this game.

When you go back to your desk after a good round of "Ain't It Awful," what happens? You're even more annoyed. The work you're supposed to do seems more unreasonable. Your boss's words and behavior seem dumber and meaner. Your whole outlook about your job is worse than it was before you got in this self-defeating game.

The point? Don't play. Stay away from people who want to help you feel worse. Maybe you'll feel left out by your peers for a while, but soon you'll be feeling better about yourself. And believe it or not, chances are you'll like your job more too.

Other Stupid Games

Here's another game some people play: It's called "If Only."

If only my boss realized how much work I already have to do.

If only my boss appreciated what I'm doing.

If only I had a different boss!

This negative game leads to two more related gambits called "Why?" and "When Things Are Different."

"Why?" goes like this: "Why does he always do that?" Do you really want to know why? I doubt it. What you really mean is that you don't like that she does that. "Why?" is a complaint masquerading as a question.

"When Things Are Different" is a form of unrealistic bargaining and it's played like this:

"When I get a raise, I'll do the kind of report they're asking for."

"When they give me the respect I deserve, then I'll come to work smiling."

"When they step up to the plate, I'll step up. That's when I'll start working harder."

Really? The trouble is there's always a new "when." The only thing that happens is, you never allow yourself a chance to actually accomplish anything. What these games do is take you away from where you are and what you're doing. They take you away from the here and now and put your attention on the evils of the past or a fantasy of the future. You've become passive in the present. And the ironic thing is, this is the only present there is! But that doesn't bother a true gamer. It's not your fault. It's not your responsibility.

In football, none of these games are allowed into the locker room or on the field. If players have these tendencies, they keep them to themselves. A dissenting voice on a team isn't tolerated for long. In this way, football has an advantage over life in the corporate world.

> Identify your issues, put together a constructive game plan with solutions, and present them to your boss.

Football players don't need to play these games, because (are you ready?) football is already a game!

So, since none of the games I've described do you any good, why play them? Whose life is it? Who's the unhappy one and who is causing this unhappiness? It's your life and you're the one who's suffering. So do something about it! Identify your issues, put together a constructive game plan with solutions, and present them to your boss.

Your Boss is Human

In my seminars on this subject, people often ask how you combat these negative thoughts and feelings.

To start, I suggest that you remember your boss is a human being. Your boss is probably a lot like you, with ambitions, career goals, financial needs, a home, a family. She wakes up cranky some days. He wakes up on top of the world some days. She has weaknesses, uncertainties, "hot buttons," ego, very much like you do.

And consider this for a moment: your boss has a boss. A boss who's very likely even more unreasonable to your boss than your boss is to you!

For one thing, admitting your boss is human makes you and your boss equals in the grand scheme of things. It levels the playing field, as the saying goes.

Realizing that your boss is only human is the critical first step in successfully managing him or her. The second step is to figure out what your boss's priorities and goals are. When you know that, you can prioritize your own work to meet your boss's goals.

Here's an important note. When you took this job, you probably got some sort of job description, either written or oral. You probably had the impression that the job description was what you were hired to do. Wrong. The job description described a general position in an otherwise mythical company. What you were truly hired to do is a lot more. And that's not always easy to figure out. So...

Find Out the Boss's Priorities

How do you find out what the boss's priorities and goals are? How do you find out what anyone's are? Here's how: Once upon a time, you were

> Teachers got students to pay attention to what they were saying by putting it on the test. In adult life, the "test" is about money, happiness, freedom, or power.

in 3rd grade, sitting at your little desk, listening to your teacher drone on and on, boring you to sleep. Suddenly, an obnoxious kid in the back of the room yells out, "Hey teacher, is this gonna be on the test?"

You were embarrassed to hear someone actually ask that question. Everyone avoided eye contact with the teacher. But you listened very carefully to the answer. If the answer was, "No, but it's something interesting I want you all to remember," your reaction was ho-hum, tune out, pencil down, relax. It's not on the test. But if the teacher said, "Yes. This will be a very important part of the test," you straightened up and started taking notes. "Can I borrow a pencil? What was that?" You paid attention because it was going to be on the test!

Thanks to those childhood days, a lot of people do only what they perceive to be "on the test." They do only the stuff that promotes or satisfies their interests in some way. In school, the motivation was grades. Teachers got students to pay attention to what they were saying by putting it on the test. In adult life, the "test" is about money, happiness, freedom, or power.

> Since the only thing people want to know is whether something's on the test, find out if what the boss assigns you to do is ON THE TEST!

So, since the only thing people want to know is whether something's on the test, find out if what the boss assigns you to do is ON THE TEST!

How do you find out? Sometimes that's difficult. Your best clues are in the boss's behavior. What does he ask for most often? What does she criticize most often? What angers him? What makes her smile or give out a compliment?

If you're not sure what's on the boss's test, what else can you do? Simple. Ask. But be forewarned. Some bosses don't like being asked. Some bosses aren't always sure what they want. And some bosses don't know how to communicate what they want. In those cases, it's up to you to figure out what the boss wants. And there is a tricky interim step to this process. It's calculating the difference between what the boss wants and what the boss needs. Once you've guessed your best guess, put it in writing in a short memo or proposal, and see how your boss responds.

Ultimately, you stand a much better chance of getting what you want if you give the boss what she wants. That brings up the simple key to

> Just say "yes." Once you've made it clear that you're willing and eager to do what the boss has asked, then you can explain the difficulties and conflicts.

successfully managing the boss. Just say "yes." Once you've made it clear that you're willing and eager to do what the boss has asked, then you can explain the difficulties and conflicts. Give the boss a choice. Bosses don't like excuses. They don't want to hear the reasons you can't or don't want to do something. They want to hear "Yes." So give them "Yes." Then they can calm down and you can give them the rest: the other things you've got to finish, the equipment or data you need to do what they've asked. Now you've given the boss a choice.

Lose the Negativity

Bosses want to deal with you without worrying about you. You need

VALUABLE LESSON	
#9	You need to be in charge of your own confidence.

to be in charge of your own confidence. Listen to how you talk to yourself. "You stupid idiot. You shouldn't have done that!" or "You loser. This is no good" or "You really fouled up this time. Try not being such a dork for a change!" Or worse.

Now, really. Stop for a minute. IF SOMEONE TALKED TO YOU THE WAY YOU TALK TO YOURSELF, YOU'D NEVER SPEAK TO THEM AGAIN. (This was a sign on my desk for years!)

Those nasty ways you talk to yourself are defeatist. They tear away at your self-esteem. They make you defensive and insecure. They put you in a position to argue, talk back, and be a victim.

Keep watch on those self-defeating thoughts and get rid of them. They are not you. When one of those self-defeating thoughts comes

> If someone talked to you the way you talk to yourself, you'd never speak to them again.

along, step back, take a look at it, blow your internal whistle (See Chapter 24: Time Out: Blowing Your Internal Whistle). You have one, just like the referee on the field. Blow it before you do any damage, before you turn yourself into a victim. The point? You can't manage anyone else until you first learn how to manage yourself. Avoid the victimizing sideline games and go for the plays that will score, for both your boss and yourself.

VALUABLE LESSON
#10 You can't manage anyone else until you first learn how to manage yourself. Avoid the victimizing sideline games and go for the plays that will score, for both your boss and yourself.

Managers don't just delegate then disappear. They monitor the activity, and respond and react. They respond to the way you say and do things. *Your* attitude and *your* behavior control at least half of the management flow. And that means *you* can manage your manager.

Which is another way of saying *you* can coach the coach!

CHAPTER  8

QUARTERBACKING YOUR LIFE: JUST SAY NO TO PUNTING

"The objective is for the quarterback — the field general — to be on target as he marches his troops into enemy territory, balancing an aerial assault with a sustained ground attack which punches holes in the forward wall of the enemy's lines. In baseball the object is to go home! And be safe!"
–George Carlin

On the football field, the quarterback is the leader of the team. He needs to stay cool in the midst of chaos. He needs to be calm despite the presence of several 280-pound linebackers whose only intent is to knock him down. The quarterback needs to be collected while everything around him is in turmoil, and he needs to do all of this while demonstrating leadership, passion, and swagger.

You Are the Field General

From calling the plays to calling the signals and changing the play at the line of scrimmage, you need to keep a cool head. You know that being flexible and spontaneous helps you keep it together in a clutch play. And when or if your protection breaks down, you have to be able to take the hit and get back up so you can reassert your dominance in the very next moment. It's not enough for you to play. You have to lead.

You're the leader of your own life. "What kind of life are you leading?" or "That person led a good life." These are comments we've all heard.

You are the only leader your life has or will ever have. It's you and no one else. It's not always a case of whether you're doing a good or bad job of it. That's not the issue. It's your job to take control of your life (or that of your team), and with that assignment comes a certain amount of responsibility. Once you establish yourself as the leader of your life, you'll discover how natural it feels and how much you like it. The better it feels, the more you'll want to do it. This is why no quarterback EVER wants to retire!

> Once you establish yourself as the leader of your life, you'll discover how natural it feels and how much you like it. This is why no quarterback EVER wants to retire!

Once you've started leading your life, once you've become your own quarterback, once you're playing a more active role in making your life more fulfilling, interesting and satisfying things start to happen. There are parallels between football and life: In areas where you're weak, you look for help and support. In the places where you're strong, you build on that strength to become more powerful. Your ultimate goal is making your strengths the source of your livelihood and emotional satisfaction.

> Be your own quarterback. Take charge. Use your support team as your blockers. Lead your life. Charge!

There's a reason the quarterback is generally regarded as the most important position on the field — it's because he's in charge.

We usually don't have an option in business or relationships to punt our responsibilities down the field or away from our immediate attention. As a last resort, we can hand the ball (or responsibility) to someone who is capable. But, mostly we have to take the ball in our own hands and power through the line. In football it's called a quarterback sneak. The quarterback takes the ball and moves it forward on the ground, using his blockers to clear a small path.

Be your own quarterback. Take charge. Use your support team as your blockers. Lead your life. Charge!

VALUABLE LESSON	
#11	There are parallels between football and life: In areas where you're weak, you look for help and support. In the places where you're strong, you build on that strength to become more powerful. Your ultimate goal is making your strengths the source of your livelihood and emotional satisfaction.

CHAPTER 9

NO FLAGS: KEEP IT IN YOUR POCKET

"The game should be called 'Feetball': where your feet are is as important to watch as the ball."
–Jim Tunney

In everyday life we tend to focus on the content of what people say and do (the ball). But sometimes intention counts for a lot.

In any football game, referees are going to call penalties. They throw a yellow scarf down onto the field. Statistically speaking, the team with fewer penalties is usually the team that wins. On the field, a penalty will move a team backward from 5 to 15 yards, depending on the severity of the misdeed. A pass interference flag can cost a team between 30 and 50 yards, because the referee brings the ball forward to the point of the interference. That could be half the field!

Don't Retaliate

And remember, in football, it's not always the player who throws the first punch who gets flagged for fighting. Usually, it's the player who punches back. He's the one who gets caught. It's not technically fair, but that's the way it works. 95% of flags thrown in an on-field fight are thrown against the player who retaliated. The penalty is called "unnecessary roughness." This can cost your team 15 yards. In football, there are some standards that coaches impart to their players to avoid fights or fouls. Be mature. Blow your internal whistle. DON'T retaliate. The most important principle is SHAKE IT OFF. Don't let your mistake affect your next play. A "late hit" or revenge move on an opponent can cost the team another 15 yards.

My friend and fellow speaker, Jim Tunney, a former NFL official, told me that fouls are committed for two reasons: 1) lack of preparation, and 2) anticipation. Jim says true leadership is staying in the moment, for players and referees alike. At all times, the player needs to know where his feet and body are on the field. A false start results when a player moves too early. The referee also cannot anticipate. Before the referee calls a penalty, he needs to make sure he reads the play correctly and THEN makes the call.

VALUABLE LESSON	
#12	Fouls are committed for two reasons: 1) lack of preparation, and 2) anticipation. True leadership is staying in the moment

Pick Your Battles

> It's a mistake to throw a flag on every little infraction a family member, coworker, or your boss may make. Pick your battles carefully.

Just as in a football game there are penalties in everyday life, too. People sometimes unwittingly say things that are hurtful. Disparaging tones of voice may creep into a conversation. But it's a mistake to throw a flag on every little infraction a family member, co-worker, or your boss may make. Pick your battles carefully. Your restraint will serve you well.

When you make a conscious choice about what you'll do instead of slipping into a knee-jerk reaction, you have more control over your behavior. When or if you do decide to get into someone's face about an infraction or disagreement, you can make it count. When you think ahead and handle conflicts with skill, you have the luxury of knowing that the ensuing confrontation may be well worth it. To get the results you want you have to know what you're talking about. Don't waste energy on small, petty issues. Only address situations that truly matter.

If you end up overstepping your bounds and you have a flag thrown on you, try to take it in stride. During a game, players and coaches are allowed to ask for an explanation of a penalty, but if they argue too much, they risk being thrown out of the game. So, make an effort to interpret your penalty from the other's point of view. You already know it doesn't work to get defensive or try to cut down the other party. You end up with the real issue being ignored and nobody wins. Pretend you have only so many penalty flags. Be careful not to use them all up.

VALUABLE LESSON	
#13	When you think ahead and handle conflicts with skill, you have the luxury of knowing that the ensuing confrontation may be well worth it.

Even better advice: Keep the flag in your pocket. We all know that life isn't fair, and sometimes we get the brunt of someone else's ill will. It doesn't always work to fight back, to accuse, or especially, to try and pay back. When we do need to confront an issue, it helps to have a clear head and some perspective so we don't exacerbate the situation. And there are times when it just isn't worth it. Why waste time on the small stuff? That might be a moment when we just have to pick up our flag, dust it off, and move on.

ATTITUDE: A LITTLE THING CALLED CHARACTER

"Always keep an open mind and a compassionate heart."
–Phil Jackson

CHAPTER  10

COMMIT: DO OR DIE

"You don't have to explain victory, and you can't explain defeat."
—Darrell Royal, Hall of Fame College football coach.

"You either have what you want, or the reasons why you don't."
—Werner Erhard

No Quitting

To achieve most things in life, even small ones, but especially big ones, you have to have commitment and discipline. Commitment is the will to see your objective realistically and dedicate your time and energy to it. Discipline is the act of carrying this out. And you cannot quit.

My mother taught me never quit. It was the Illinois High School State Speech Tournament. It was my senior year, and my school, Richwoods Community High School of Peoria, was in the finals. I was in the middle of my comedy reading event in a very hot, packed classroom, when I went blank. The silence scared me and I felt faint. I stumbled toward the door, opened it, and felt a whoosh of cool air. My mother was right behind me.

She said, "Miriam, get back in there and finish!"

"No, Mom, I can't; I'm too embarrassed," I said.

Mom said, "We don't quit; get back in there." I flashed her a look; she was being rough on me, but it was necessary. And she recited the last line of the routine I had uttered. I went back in, fought through the waves of pity I felt from the audience, and made them laugh once more. The judges gave me fifth place which counted for one point for my team. That year, my school won its first State Championship by... one point. Really. If I had quit, I would not have been awarded that one point, and we would not have won. That's how important it was for me not to quit.

Professional football players come with commitment and discipline and no quitting already installed in their systems. They would have never been able to get into the NFL without these characteristics. No one makes it into professional sports without them.

And in the world of business, the ones who succeed usually have the same kind of commitment and discipline as their athletic counterparts. In fact, you will often find that these business leaders are also big sports fans, as well as being very competitive athletes in their own right. These principles are that universal. Success in the boardroom often walks hand-in-hand with success on the field.

Commitment: My Definition

You may be saying to yourself as you read this, "If only I had that kind of commitment and discipline. Maybe then I would be more successful." It's a lament I often hear when I address various groups, companies, and organizations during my training sessions. That's when I offer *MY* definition of commitment: "If you don't achieve your objective, someone will cut off the index finger of your writing hand below the second knuckle."

This definition, which sounds a wee bit harsh, grew out of a discussion with a resistant participant in a team-building seminar. She insisted she had done all the right things, and the "other guy" was late delivering a report due to her every Thursday by 5:00 pm. The "other guy" was a co-worker in another department and she depended on his information.

I said to her, "What do you do at 5:01 pm on Thursday when you haven't gotten the report?" She said, "Well, I call him Friday morning and..."

I said, "Friday? What about Thursday? You need it Thursday!" Just as I suspected, she called Friday to chastise him for not turning in the report. She was one of those people who prefer to have reasons for not getting a job done rather than doing whatever it takes to get it done.

I was so frustrated by her defeatist attitude that I spontaneously shot her this question: "What if the index finger of your right hand will be cut off at 5:01 on Thursday if you don't have the report from him?" Her entire demeanor changed. I was rough, but it was necessary. She thought for a moment and said, "Well, I guess if it was *that* serious, I might tell him that the report was due on Wednesday."

The other participants vocalized approval and a couple of them even applauded. Then she started really getting into the exercise. She said, "Not only would I tell him it was due on Wednesday, but I would probably be a lot nicer to him."

The class exploded in approving "wup-wups." One guy said, "Yeah,

> If the stakes are high enough, you change your behavior, even if it means taking extra steps. That's commitment.

you would probably want to know who was in charge of the material for his report in case he died before 5:00 on Thursday." Big laughs. Then another person said, "I would visit his office, ask about his kids, and make sure that the material for my report is in a fireproof filing cabinet." More laughs. The class was beginning to get the meaning of *commitment.* If the stakes are high enough, you change your behavior, even if it means taking extra steps. That's commitment. Feedback after the seminar indicated that, even with the people who seem most impossible, you can get what you want if you are committed to doing whatever it takes to get results.

Commitment: The Football Lesson

Just as a football player has to muster the commitment and discipline to pursue athletic excellence on the field, so must you. The football player's motivation is simple: There are thousands of guys out there who would sell their souls for a chance at his spot. He HAS to be excellent. In your chosen field of endeavor, you can operate from that principle, too. You need to have commitment and discipline.

When a football player isn't doing one of his practice drills just so, the coach will make him do it again and again and again, until the player gets it right. No excuses, no reasons why he cannot do it. Maybe the same kind of approach would work for you. Are you having trouble with commitment and discipline? The next time you face a task or chore you find difficult, you can come up with reasons why you cannot do it OR you can do whatever it takes to get it done. That's commitment.

VALUABLE LESSON	
#14	The next time you face a task or chore you find difficult, you can come up with reasons why you cannot do it OR you can do whatever it takes to get it done. That's commitment.

CHAPTER 11

MAN UP: OR "WELCOME TO QUEBEC!"

"Rejection is just missing success by about a hair or two."
—Herm Edwards, from the book, It's the Will,
Not the Skill, by Jim Tunney

In the preseason, before the first regular game, players are vying for a spot on the team. All the coaches must get together to reduce the roster from 80 to 53 players. It's a brutal process, and the player who is "cut" has to "man up" in the face of this otherwise humiliating rejection.

Rejection: Learn to Live with It

Life has lots of rejections along its path, from little everyday things, to big life-changing things. This is true of football as well. Players put up with rejections on and off the field. Let's look at one example.

A team with a star running back is on the field. The running back is not having a great game. Doesn't matter why; he's just having an off day. It happens. His pace is a split second slow. His vision isn't as precise. He can't hit the hole (the gap between players) as fast or hard as he usually does.

What happens?

The coach turns to his second best running back. All of a sudden, the #2 guy is getting handed the ball a little more than usual. Maybe he can make something happen. #1 feels rejected. But he still has a part to play. He's still in the game. He can still contribute. So, he shifts his focus accordingly and helps #2 carry the ball and maybe carry the game. That's what a team player does. He doesn't whine and complain about not getting the ball. He makes the most out of his circumstance and sets his mind to playing hard, all in the face of having been rejected.

I learned a long time ago that I hate rejection. I had a phone sales job and with every rejection, I'd go to the vending machine and buy a candy bar. Two weeks and six pounds later, I could no longer button my clothes. I had to quit.

Years later on the phone, selling my own training courses, I felt the same resistance to hearing "no" when I was trying to close the deal. I found myself more satisfied with "I want to think it over." I preferred to accept a prospect's indecision rather than close the deal with "no." I had a six-inch stack of incomplete files on potential clients. I was spending many hours following up on these people, only to hear "Maybe. Call me in a couple of months." Not as good as "Yes," but better than "No." I had been calling some people for over two years! It was time to find a new approach.

Last Call at the Bar

So I called *one last time* and told them this was their final call. It was like giving them last call at the bar. After the initial small talk, I said, "I'm cleaning up my files and closing some of them. We've been talking for over a year, and I've yet to arrange a training program for your staff. This will be my last call to you. It's like last call at the bar at closing time. *Really*, what are the chances of getting to work for you and train your people?"

And then I listened. The results amazed me.

About a third of the prospects sounded relieved. They said they didn't think there was much chance: no budget, they didn't believe in training, they already use someone else — all useful, informative facts I *needed* to know in order to stop wasting my time and money calling unqualified buyers!

Another third were like the people at the bar: ordering that last drink just in case they would need it. They made appointments on the spot to schedule a meeting with me or promised to talk to their boss on my behalf.

And the final third managed to convince me to hang on and keep following up, which I was willing to do, because now my unclosed stack was much smaller. What a great feeling closure is, even when the closure is "No."

Be proactive. Ask for a decision.

Don't let rejection waste your time, money, and other valuable resources. Be like the running back: get back in the game, and help your team win.

VALUABLE LESSON	
#15	Don't let rejection waste your time, money, and other valuable resources. Be like the running back: get back in the game, and help your team win.

CHAPTER  12

STAY LIGHT ON YOUR FEET: REVERSES, SCRAMBLING, AND OTHER BROKEN PLAYS

"Champions keep playing until they get it right "
–Billie Jean King

Do More with Less

Every football season it's the same old story. Players leave the team; new players come in. And the returning players face this changeover with a small measure of dread. Why? They anticipate the same thing you do whenever someone is laid off in your department: they will be expected to pick up the slack. They will be asked to do more with less.

When a quarterback loses his two favorite receivers, one being traded to another team, the other retiring from the game altogether, he stares down an uncertain future with two new guys. Will they perform? If they do, will it be at the same level as the outgoing stars? How am I going to do more with less? The one comfort in football is, they will never downsize the team. There will always be 11 guys on each side, but their skills will be at different levels.

But in your case, they may not replace your outgoing co-workers. They lay off two workers and only hire one. Now, everybody in the department presumably gets to share the pain. How do you do it?

Here's how: You stay light on your feet. You go with the flow. You may not think you like your new and expanded duties, but that doesn't mean you can't do them well. You don't always have to like something to be good at it. And if you're good at it, you can get it done more quickly and not have to worry about it. That's staying light on your feet.

Here's another way: Try to group your similar tasks together. If location plays a part in your responsibilities, do all the things that happen in a specific place while you're at that place. Or if your new duties utilize similar skills, do them concurrently. You might find that you can sandwich your new tasks in between your existing tasks without a lot more time and effort. Do more with less by staying light on your feet.

VALUABLE LESSON	
#16	The worker who can do more with less will be first in line when it's time to move up!

And remember: the worker who can do more with less will be first in line when it's time to move up!

Change Sucks; Deal with It

The simple fact remains: Change sucks.

We resist it. Even good change rates high on the stress scale.

We don't like it at home. We don't like it at work. We think it's unfair and that it shouldn't happen. We use it as an excuse for not trying.

Before we start to gripe, we should find out if the change is going to benefit us. If it is, we need to shut up! If it isn't, we need to do what football teaches us: Adapt, Improvise, Overcome. That's what it's all about.

If you can approach change with a mind to Adapt, Improvise, and Overcome, you won't resist change so much.

But in football, change is inevitable. Not only season to season, but sometimes in the middle of the season. Sometimes (gasp!), in the middle of the darn game! Horrors! What shall we do? Stand around and whine like a bunch of babies? Or get on with the tasks at hand and go win a football game?

Head coaches come and go. Recently, almost a dozen first-time head coaches were helming teams. That's a third of the entire league. Key players retire, get replaced, or suffer career-ending injuries. Not only does the team have to Adapt, Improvise, and Overcome, but think about the poor player.

VALUABLE LESSON	
#17	If you can approach change with a mind to Adapt, Improvise, and Overcome, you won't resist change so much.

What the heck is he gonna do? Football may be all he knows!

Even owners change. The old guy who bought the franchise back in 1959 dies. His son takes over. Or the team is sold. New regime is in place.

All these examples serve us well in the real world. Gone are the days of the gold watch for a lifetime of service with one company. These days, people average three to five career changes in their lifetime. So it's time to learn the football lesson: Adapt, Improvise, Overcome. You don't have to like change. But you can't afford not to do it well.

Here's an example of a change that no one liked, but everyone in football now accepts.

In the late 1990s, the NFL introduced the concept of parity: the team with the worst record would have first pick in the draft the following year. The second worst team record would get second pick, and so on. At first, it seemed like a stupid idea (except to last year's last place teams!). Then everyone gradually started to see the benefits of it. The result? It's added another vital dimension to the game by keeping teams more equal and competition more fierce.

The best way to deal with change is the same way you deal with an oncoming defensive lineman: stay light on your feet.

CHAPTER 13

HAVE A THICK SKIN: SHUT UP AND GET OVER IT

"Sports do not build character. They reveal it."
–John Wooden

The reason football players wear helmets and pads is obvious. They don't want to get hurt. Since the game inherently comes with a certain degree of physicality, the best way to deal with it is a very simple solution: an extra layer of protection around your body. And it mostly works. Yes, there are still many injuries in football, in ALL sports. But the advances in football protection get better every year.

Life, like football, is a contact sport. It comes with bumps and bruises. Emotionally speaking, life can rough you up. That's why it's good to have an extra layer of emotional protection around your body. We're talking about an emotional buffer zone, a coating, a shield. And just

> Life, like football, is a contact sport. It comes with bumps and bruises.

like football, your pads should not hamper your mobility and speed. You may still get tackled and taken to the ground, but you'll be more equipped to get back up and be ready for the next play.

The great thing about football helmets and pads is they're built for comfort. Hard on the outside and soft on the inside. That's a good way to be.

No Complaining

To wrap yourself in emotional protection, spend a moment doing some internal soul-searching before displaying your raw feelings to the outside world. Players (people) who complain the most about life tend to be the ones that get tackled more often. Avoid being that person. No one likes a whiner. Same for people on the field of life. Players who whine need thicker pads. Now, more than ever, you have to be mentally tough to survive. You have to be able to say "So what!"

> Players (people) who complain the most about life tend to be the ones that get tackled more often.

This is an especially popular refrain on the gridiron. Football professionals have to be more than physically tough; they have to be mentally tough as well, AND they have to do it while the whole world watches.

Vince Young Learns a Lesson

In the Tennessee Titans 2008 opening game, the Titans quarterback, Vince Young, left the field after a bad play to the sound of unfamiliar boos. A few minutes later, in the next series he injured his left knee, and the camera caught him rolling helplessly around on the field.

Young, in his third season and a former NFL Offensive Rookie of the Year, didn't show up the next day for an MRI on his knee. The day after, the coach came to his house. Vince said he didn't want to play anymore because he was

VALUABLE LESSON	
#18	When you get booed, you need to shut up and get over it.

hurt from the boos. He didn't want to play anymore for the rest of the season.

Time passed and Vince Young learned when you get booed, you need to shut up and get over it. Now his career is going very well.

Failing: Not All Bad

These days, we need to give kids the opportunity to experience defeat. Parents have become afraid to let their kids fail because they fear their precious little ones suffer damaged self-esteem. Kids get a trophy for just showing up. Parents have forgotten that failure NEEDS to happen for kids to achieve happiness and success! Failing to win, with the help of comforting hugs from parents, leads to a thick skin. Kids know the game has some necessary roughness, as does life. Successful football players, as well as entrepreneurs and successful people everywhere, know this.

An especially effective way to deal with life's bumps and bruises is to develop the ultimate set of pads. Having a thick skin and not complaining is vital for your success in the business world and in your relationships. I don't know if he was a fan of American football, but Winston Churchill said, "Success consists of going from failure to failure without loss of enthusiasm." This is a guy who always strapped on his helmet and pads. And he'd have made a helluva head coach!

VALUABLE LESSON	
#19	Winston Churchill said, "Success consists of going from failure to failure without loss of enthusiasm."

CHAPTER  14

THAT LITTLE VOICE INSIDE YOUR HELMET: AND IT'S NOT THE COACH

"Our life is frittered away by detail. Simplify, SIMPLIFY."
–Henry David Thoreau

Football is a demanding game.

All players have to be in excellent physical shape.

All players have to be mentally focused.

All players have to be instilled with a passion for winning.

But the truly great players throughout the decades bring something else to the game. They bring a knowing. Somehow, they have an additional sense about the nature of the game. It's often called instinct. Coaches love players with good instincts. They try to help players develop these instincts. But it's not an easy thing to teach.

So, as players in the game of life, how do we cultivate our instincts?

We listen to our inner voice.

Your Inner Voice

Do you have an inner voice? Have you ever listened to your inner voice? Yes, it's that little voice that just said, "What little voice?"

I remember the first time I heard my inner voice. This voice sounded different from the chatter of my usual critical judging about what people looked like, what they were saying, how they sounded. It was calm and quiet, and it had a knowing about it.

It was 1982, around Mile 8 of a ten-mile run during my training regimen for my first marathon race. It was the longest run I had ever attempted, and I could hear my thoughts slowing down. I was grappling with a knotty problem I faced with a friend of mine. My inner voice slowly started talking to my friend with understanding and a patient tone. Suddenly, I knew I

VALUABLE LESSON	
#20	How do we cultivate our instincts? We listen to our inner voice.

was listening to the words I would need to resolve our conflict. I realized that using my instinct, the situation could be settled. Athletes say it was the extra adrenaline pumping through my system from running, giving me an endorphin high. Endorphins relieve pain and allow mental facility. In football, it often gives brute strength.

We can get the strength of calm wisdom from our inner voice for our work and our relationships. Now I hear my inner voice when I'm sitting still.

At first, I thought I needed a beautiful place, like the beach or the mountains to hear it. And I thought I had to be alone. But as time went on, I found I could hear my inner voice anywhere, even walking up and down the supermarket aisles!

Write it Down

Sometimes, my inner voice wakes me up in the early morning hours. So, I reach for the pad on my night table and write what it says without editing. Then I go back to sleep. When I wake up and read what I've written, I can hear my inner voice again, and my notes make sense. That's how I came up with the title of this book — at 5:18 am on August 18, 2009.

I've gotten so good at it I can summon it by simply asking myself a question internally and just listening to the answer. It's become a habit.

If I had a football coach, he'd be pleased.

ACHIEVEMENT: THE HALL OF FAME

"You gotta believe to achieve."
  –Mike Ditka

CHAPTER  15

THE SIX M'S: THE ROAD MAP TO YOUR HALL OF FAME

"Each trophy signified a dream come true, someone's potential tested to its limit."
—Rick Telander, from his book, Like a Rose.

How can football help you in the pursuit of your goals?

Let's take a look at a player who has been used sparingly on the field. He's a second-stringer, a bench-warmer. Every team has these guys. He plays only when a starting player goes down. Maybe he starts on Special Teams.

In some cases, that's okay. That's where he wants to stay. He's fine just being a part of the world's most elegant war game. He simply wants to play his part and go home at the end of the day. No problem.

But for a guy who wants to become a starter, it's a different story.

> Being a starter is as good as it gets. And it doesn't just happen.

Being a starter is as good as it gets. If you're on the starting squad, you've made it to the top of the top. That's a big deal. And it doesn't just happen. To make it happen, whether he's a rookie or a veteran player, he needs to get his mind right. He needs to tap into a concept I call conscious competence.

> "With luck, anyone can sell anything to anyone once. Doing it twice takes more than luck. It takes skill."

My grandfather, who was a salesman, used to say, "With luck, anyone can sell anything to anyone once. Doing it twice takes more than luck. It takes skill." That skill is conscious competence: the awareness of the process that allowed you to make the first sale so you can repeat it.

Conscious Competence

Conscious competence works for sales. And it works for everything else.

VALUABLE LESSON
#21 Starting a business, moving up the corporate ladder, retaining your client base, taking your business to the next level are all like starting a long run. Each takes discipline and commitment over time. And discipline and commitment over time is what leads to conscious competence.

As I wrote earlier, in 1983 I ran a marathon. It was then I coined the concept of conscious competence. It was part of my mind-set as I approached the training process. Because a marathon is 26.2 miles long, running that distance is not something you can just "do." It takes discipline and commitment over time.

You must run a certain number of miles every week to condition your body to avoid injury. I started with half a block. Then I ran a full block, then two, building up. If I didn't feel like running, I still ran. If it was drizzling outside, I still ran. If I wasn't in the mood, guess what? Unless I was flat on my back in bed with a high fever, I ran. You run whether you feel like it or not. That is what discipline and commitment demand.

Starting a business, moving up the corporate ladder, retaining your client base, taking your business to the next level are all like starting a long run. Each takes discipline and commitment over time. And discipline and commitment over time is what leads to conscious competence.

My Hall of Fame

In my Hall of Fame you get inducted by following the Six M's. These six concepts are the cornerstones for building a strong foundation for success. If you can master the Six M's, there is nothing you can't accomplish. This is what conscious competence is all about.

Pittsburgh had The Steel Curtain. Minnesota had The Purple People Eaters. Dallas had The Doomsday Defense. Each of these squads made a name for themselves as a group, and each guy was necessary for the group's success. That's how I feel about the 6 M's. They are a team and they work together. That's where they get their strength.

Owners, executives, managers, bosses, workers, and employees of companies large and small will find ideas within the 6 M's that resonate with them. So will football players who want to be on the starting team. These

MISSION, MOTIVATE, MARKET, MANAGE, MENTOR, and MEASURE.

six simple concepts working together can power up every one of us to control our own destiny in the workplace or on the gridiron.

The Six M's you need to activate are: MISSION, MOTIVATE, MARKET, MANAGE, MENTOR, and MEASURE. Let's take a look at each one of these.

CHAPTER  16

KNOW YOUR MISSION

"When you follow your bliss... doors will open where you
would not have thought there would be doors."
–Joseph Campbell

In the case of our football player, he already knows what his mission is. He wants to be the best player at his position on his team. That's his path to becoming a starter.

VALUABLE LESSON	
#22	Just as most companies have a mission statement, you need to have one, too.

Just as most companies have a mission statement, you need to have one, too. Your mission statement is a description of the future that you see for yourself. It is a clear, understandable, concise, and descriptive statement. It may contain needs you want to fill, whom you want to have as your primary clients, how you want to conduct your business, and other such principles.

What is Your Mission?

Your mission may be your reason for living. And it may be what you would do anyway, even for no pay. Your mission is based on your values, the principles by which you live your life. Some of my values are: integrity, trust, respect, contribution, growth.

What is your ongoing, overall purpose in life?

My mission statement is: "To assist people to realize and achieve their full human potential." These are the words that light my fire each morning and I feel lucky to love what I do.

Some of us are blessed to be doing what we love. My brother-in-law, a successful sales executive in the insurance and financial services industry, is one such person. His business mission has always been: "To continue to grow as a person while helping others to grow, enthusiastically!" Your mission statement may be: "To provide a more favorable financial future for my clients."

> Your mission statement determines what you consider worthy of your commitment and justifies the accompanying discipline you need to achieve it.

Are you in sales? Think about what you sell. My brother-in-law sells insurance. But let's relate it to his mission; he sells life enhancement products that elevate people's lives by creating a secure financial future for them. These kinds of words are likely to help you aspire to something loftier than merely pushing a product. They are an expression of something greater. They are your mission.

If you are a receptionist, you give the first impression people receive of the company. Your mission may be: "To recognize and respond to each visitor so they feel respected upon arrival."

Corporate mission statements may help you to identify your own mission. Some examples are: "To generate products in a morally acceptable manner within a sufficient time frame." Another: "To provide service and products that care about people." And another: "To improve people's lives by advancing information storage and access to help the world remember."

How to Write Your Mission

To determine your mission statement, ask yourself some key questions:

- What did you want to be when you grew up? What traits did you associate with that profession?

- What are the five values most important to you? What are the five values least important to you?

- What do you do well?

- What is your unique contribution to the world?

- What positive things have people said to you? Clients are usually more eloquent about us than we ourselves can be. Make notes about what your clients have said about you. Do people thank you for following up? Your clients know follow-up means you care. If you are in sales, think about your last sale. What did your buyer thank you for? What did the person in the next department thank you for?

- Is your life mission statement different from your job mission statement? If so, how?

Just like a football player looking to be Top Dog, your mission statement determines what you consider worthy of your commitment and justifies the accompanying discipline you need to achieve it, grueling though it may be.

CHAPTER 17

MOTIVATE YOURSELF

"There's no substitute for guts."
–Bear Bryant

The football player has it easier than we do on this one. His motivation is his desire to be a starter. Other factors can play into that. Maybe he wants more money. Or a better contract. Or more security. Or maybe he just wants the championship! That's cool. Why not? That will surely get a guy off his butt in pursuit of it!

For us, it's a bit trickier. But we can start by setting daily goals. Be realistic. You can reach five potential clients. Maybe not twenty-five!

In football, the coaching staff provides these goals for him. But a smart coach also provides another motivator — a reward. So, motivating yourself also means rewarding yourself.

What Motivates You?

I love watching television. I've always loved it. When I started

Motivating yourself also means rewarding yourself.

my business, I worked from home — a studio apartment. The television was right there in my "office," and I made marketing phone calls during the commercials. Today, I would never think of turning on the television during the work day. However, I am still the same person motivated by the same things. I set a goal of a certain number of calls and appointments and promise myself a reward when I reach the goal: my favorite TiVo'd TV show.

You need to discover what motivates you to make the calls, to be the disciplined person. It may be an afternoon movie, a day at the park, or a massage. Be careful if you just thought about Haagen-Dazs. For some of us, ice cream is a double-edged sword. It might not be so rewarding long term.

Most of the time, you can be enthusiastic because you like what you do. But what if you don't feel like it one day? Then what do you do?

What If You Don't Feel Motivated?

You fake it.

You fake it till you make it. Sometimes it's the only way to conscious competence. This is the discipline part. What about the mornings when you get up in a negative frame of mind? Before I get out of bed in the morning, I prop up (so I don't fall back to sleep) and ask myself these five morning questions:

> Fake it till you make it. Sometimes it's the only way to conscious competence.

1. What am I excited about today? Look out; the first things your mind will come up with are all the negative things you are *not* excited about: making the call to *that* person, writing *that* report, going to THAT meeting. Thank your mind politely for sharing, and ask yourself the question again. Eventually you will come up with something, even if it is: today is Friday.

2. What am I proud of today? This involves looking back into yesterday's activities. Your mind will want to bring up

regret, something you could or should have done. Definitely not something you're proud of. Again, politely thank your mind for sharing, and ask the question again. Remember, it can be as simple as being proud that you helped your assistant with the phones, while she finished a project.

3. What am I grateful for today? More is better on this one; counting your blessings can chase the blues away.

4. What am I committed to today? This is where the rubber meets the road. You need to be clear about your commitments for the day, because you will measure those results at the end of the day. This can be challenging. Some days you just don't feel like doing anything you "should." Sometimes the commitment is simply to do it anyway and fake it till you make it.

5. Who loves me? Whom do I love? I know these are two questions. I like them together. They wrap up your self-motivation session on a very upbeat note.

When I have answered these questions, I've turned my mind-set

> ## What am I committed to today? This is where the rubber meets the road.

from negative to positive. By the time my feet hit the floor, I have "hit the ground running." My head is in a positive place, and I'm ready to do positive things.

In the end, your motivation doesn't have to be noble. You can promise yourself something silly. So what? Everything doesn't have to

> ## A sloppy win is better than a pretty loss.

go exactly the way you see it in your mind. The process is allowed to be ugly. Football

players know all about ugly wins. "Whatever works" is often heard on the sidelines. There are no points given for neatness or etiquette or style. A sloppy win is better than a pretty loss.

CHAPTER  18

MARKET YOURSELF

"One is taught by experience to put a premium on those few
people who can appreciate you for what you are."
  –Gail Godwin, bestselling author and
    college friend at University of Iowa.

You are Never off the Record

This is a biggie. Not so much for our football player, but for us. Football players have agents to market them to get the job. When the player markets himself as a capable player to his coaches, the coaches will say something like: "Okay, show me!" Marketing done.

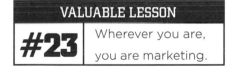

Of course, he needs to always be marketing himself to his team as a wonderful teammate.

We have to be more clever about it. You are always marketing yourself before and after you engage in an activity. People are always watching you. There is no such thing as "off the record." Marketing includes networking with others, not just calling clients or leads. Join your local Chamber of Commerce. Go to meetings. Take a class. Teach a class! And go to every networking function you can find. Once they get to know you, people do business with you. Wherever you are, you are marketing.

Does your child have a short answer to the question, "What is Mommy's job?" Can your mother or friends answer that question? Give them that short answer. Make these people your marketing partners. When my oldest nephew was five years old, he was on a soccer team. My brother-in-law, Randy, was in insurance — a hard concept for a little boy to grasp. But my brilliant brother-in-law taught Adam what Daddy did in an understandable manner. Adam told the other little boys, "My daddy makes sure your daddy has money when he's old." At the soccer games, the other fathers would sidle up to Randy and say, "Hey Randy, I hear you're going to make me money when I'm old. What do you do?" Randy sold insurance to half the team's daddys.

Marketing to friends is a special challenge. Many people feel awkward transitioning from personal to business. We fear this will impose on our friendship. For years, I did not market my services to the company where my best friend was President. Then I asked myself, "Why wouldn't I give my friend the same opportunity to experience my expertise as I give other companies?"

One day, I talked to her about it. I told her, "This is really uncomfortable for me. Yours is the only company where I personally know the President and I haven't marketed my services."

When you are true to your mission, you naturally offer your friends what you offer to strangers.

Her answer was, "That's true. What have you been working on lately?" When I told her about my courses in management, team building, and career development, she said, "This is so ironic. I have lunch with the Human Resources Director every Friday. He is your potential client, right?" She then asked for my promotional materials so she could pass them on.

When you are true to your mission, you naturally offer your friends what you offer to strangers. Talk to parents at your children's school, your neighbors, the man in line behind you at Home Depot. And remember to talk to other people in your company. They are also your partners in marketing, and you can establish strategic alliances with them. In some businesses, you may even be able to share clients and commissions.

And remember to make the process fun. Commit to five new activities you would like to pursue, such as classes in foreign language, sculpture, and writing. Then do those activities for fun. Stay open to all possibilities, and be patient. People network with those they see time and time again. As relationships grow, so can your business.

"Sell" Was a Four-Letter Word

When I first started my business, making a sales call was as difficult as training for my marathon. I was raised in a family of doctors and dentists. "Sell" was a four-letter word in our house. We knew how to *buy*. But we surely did not know how to *sell*. My mother always told me, "To succeed, just do a good job and you will be recognized. You do not need to *sell* yourself." She was half right. Doing a good job is mandatory.

> We are "selling" ourselves all the time. It's part of the game. It needs to be done. If we don't do it, no one will do it for us.

What Mom did not realize is that we are "selling" ourselves all the time. It's part of the game. It needs to be done. If we don't do it, no one will do it for us.

Cold calling is still a painful process. But I commit a certain amount of time to it — no longer than 20 minutes at a time. When I trained to run a marathon of 26.2 miles, I used to have a phrase I would tell myself to keep me going. I would think of the mile in smaller segments, and I would say, "I can do two miles more of anything." Two miles the way I jog takes about 20 minutes. When I want to quit calling, I say to myself, "I can do 20 minutes more of anything." And I keep going.

VALUABLE LESSON	
#24	Selling yourself to your boss and your team is an essential element of a successful life.

Selling yourself to your boss and your team is an essential element of a successful life. Entrepreneurs know it. Intrapreneurs (you company people) know it. And so do football players. They sell themselves, and end up endorsing products, and they make millions of dollars in the process.

CHAPTER  19

MANAGE YOUR TIME

"Until we can manage time, we can manage nothing else."
–Peter F. Drucker

How do we manage our time? Football Guy may have an easier time managing himself. He probably has people all around him who do this for him. They're called Coaches, Trainers, Agents, Lawyers, Accountants; some are even called Managers. And their job is to... manage! Brilliant.

In our case, WE are our own managers. Whether you are an entrepreneur, employee, or independent contractor, you need to manage yourself and your time. Parkinson's Law says, "Work tends to expand to the time allotted to it." So, if you have all day to write the report, how long will it take? Yes, you may stretch it out all day. But what if you have one hour to get the report done? Yes, it will take an hour.

> ## "Work tends to expand to the time allotted to it."

I believe the same rule applies to human resources: "Work tends to expand to the human resources allotted to it." You will have as much work as you can handle.

Delegate—the Magic Word

If you want to increase your work load, hire an assistant. Soon after I hired my first assistant, incoming calls doubled, then tripled. We had to send out more marketing packets and enter more names in the database. After a year, my assistant asked me, "Before I got here, how did you do all this by yourself?" I answered, "Before you got here, I didn't have all this." This follows the philosophy, "Build it and they will come." It was an important step forward for me in developing my own conscious competence (the ability to know what works so you can repeat it).

> **VALUABLE LESSON**
>
> **#25** If you want to increase your work load, hire an assistant.

A magic word in managing is delegation. It will open up extra time for you. Remember what you are paid for. I don't do anything my assistant can do. I need to market myself, so I make the phone calls. I touch people. My assistant is a computer whiz, so she touches paper/computer. That's the division of labor in our office.

> **VALUABLE LESSON**
>
> **#26** This follows the philosophy, "Build it and they will come."

Your Time Is Your Inventory

When it comes to managing your time, remember that your time is your inventory. You only have 24 hours in the day. Use it well. Be frugal. It's easy to get distracted or procrastinate. Not only time, but your energy is also your inventory. You only have so much of both. Are you frugal? Observe what you do during the day, and you can find out.

If you find yourself balancing your checkbook or looking up the latest game scores (low priorities), rather than checking your e-mail or making marketing calls (high priorities), you are sabotaging yourself. High priorities are business tasks that further your mission: answer that e-mail, research that report, make ten calls, follow up with that client again, reach that assistant at 7:00 am so you can speak to her boss. Then, later, after you've accomplished something, you can reward yourself by finding out if the San Diego Chargers won yesterday's game.

> Your time is your inventory.

Prime Time

To be a consciously competent person, schedule high priorities during prime time, the time when you are at your peak energy. Most people are either night people or morning people. Some lucky ones are both. I am a morning gal. This is great because I live on the West Coast. I can make calls to the East Coast at 6:00 am and can catch people as they start their business day. I find it energizing.

If you are a morning person, don't schedule your haircut appointment at 9:00 am. Don't file papers at 9:00 am. These are low priorities and they do not require a lot of energy. Do these when you are tired, during your lag time. Resist the seduction of doing low priorities during your prime time, just to be able to check them off. (You "check-off freaks" out there, you know who you are.) How many of you find yourselves doing something today from tomorrow's to-do list? So you write it on today's list, just so you can check it off? I used to think I was the only one, and that I was a little crazy. But, no. I find it provides us an opportunity to give ourselves props. And if we don't give those acknowledgements to ourselves, how can we expect others to do it?

Once you meet with a little success, you'll want to manage yourself

and your time even more. Clock management is basic to football. The players must excel in clock management to win. Nothing succeeds like success. I think a football guy said that.

CHAPTER  20

MENTOR: HAVE SOME AND BE ONE

"I do believe mentoring can shorten the school of hard knocks."
–Lincoln Kennedy

Have a mentor. A role model.

Be a mentor. Help someone else.

It's a two-way street. You learn and grow from both. Football players usually have a high school or college coach whom they look to as one of their first mentors. Sometimes it's a veteran player on their team they really admire, who's taken them under his wing. Whatever our football player goes on to achieve, he will almost always cite this mentor whenever he's thanking people, usually right up there with Mom and God. Good company.

Every year, at the Football Hall of Fame Induction Ceremony, the honorees are moved to tears thanking these mentors in their speech. Several honorees choose a mentor to present them first before they speak. More speeches, more tears, very schmaltzy — yet another thing we women love about football.

Pay It Forward

Our football player also pays some of his success forward. The good guys, like Lincoln Kennedy, ex-NFL Pro Bowl Offensive Lineman, and friend, will mentor younger players in the league. Lincoln says, "When we get drafted out of college, there is an invincibility factor; they tell us we are the best thing since sliced bread, and we believe it. We are 22 years old, with lots of money, and we don't have a clue what we are doing. I passed on my life lessons to younger kids and led by example. I shared my trials and tribulations and told them to shape up and move on from there."

After their careers are over and even during their careers, some NFL players and coaches start a scholarship fund for their high school football program. They will coach a local Little League team. They may set up a foundation to benefit people in need. Thus, the player or coach now becomes a mentor to folks outside the NFL.

WE CAN DO THE SAME.

To find a mentor, look for people who have what you want to have and do what you want to do. I call it a "goal model." Identify someone you can look up to, who challenges you. It's usually best to seek someone of good character, someone who shares your values and ethics. Mentors can be a support and lend a listening ear.

VALUABLE LESSON	
#28	Find a mentor, a "goal model." Identify someone you can look up to, who challenges you.

Meet them, talk to them, ask them questions. Most people respond to someone who is genuinely interested in them. To establish yourself with this mentor, don't be a pest. Identify what you want to learn from them. Tell them you honor them for their expertise. Ask how you can help them. Volunteer for tasks they need done. People tend to open up to someone offering to pitch in and help move the ball down the field.

You Learn It When You Teach It

As for mentoring, you rarely learn anything really well until you teach it. By sharing your expertise, you're forced to analyze it in a way you may never have seen it before. It makes you aware of your strengths and weaknesses. As a mentor, you control the process in the mentoring relationship. Set the agenda to include:

1. Get to know each other; build trust.
2. Discuss objectives of the relationship.
3. Set up agenda, time line, and regular meeting times.
4. Always schedule time to evaluate pluses and minuses.

Mentoring gives you a new way of approaching your own pursuits.

> When you're giving, you're getting at the same time.

You are confirming something out loud to yourself as you tell someone else, which throws a whole new light on the subject. So when you're giving, you're getting at the same time.

And you never know where your mentees will end up: Hall of Fame, Academy Awards, Nobel Prize, Mars. And they may end up thanking YOU!

CHAPTER 21

MEASURE YOUR RESULTS

"The future depends on what we do in the present."
–Mahatma Gandhi

In football, it's easy to measure. They have these little things called…
statistics! They measure EVERYTHING! So, a player or a team will
always know where they stand compared to other players and teams.
It's gotten so detailed you can sometimes hear someone quote a statistic
about a statistic. This may sound nitpicky to us, but stats have their uses.

Here are some of the things they keep track of. Passing yards.
Running yards. Total yards. The number of passes, runs, catches, touch-
downs, tackles, kicks, punts, fumbles, interceptions, and penalties.
These stats are kept according to individual players as well as teams.
They are categorized by game, week, season, and year.

In the middle of a game the sportscaster will tell you, "This is the
85th penalty this season, so this team is the 5th most penalized team in
the league." They've been keeping this stat only since 1978. Before that it
wasn't an official statistic. They keep track of how many yards a player
averages per catch. They will tell you, "This team is second in converting
3rd downs of 10 yards or more." And even though every coach, player,

commentator, and fan will tell you that stats don't win ball games, if you know how to examine them, they can help you win. That's for sure.

Tuesday Films

All NFL teams even have an extra special way to measure their performance after every game. It's affectionately called Tuesday Films. Since most games are videotaped by the networks, as well as the teams themselves, the playback of these videos provides a valuable tool in measuring a team's progress. Each team's offense and defense looks at the key plays in which they were involved. The coaches and players discuss what was done well and what wasn't, what worked and what didn't. Often, the entire team reconvenes at the end of this process so the coaching staff can play back the key plays of the overall game for further comment and analysis. Tuesday Films is a vital element in improving a team's performance. NOTE: It's called Tuesday Films because most games are played on Sunday, so Monday is a day off for most team personnel. A related statistic is that teams are in the meeting room 20 times longer than on the field for practice. Does that tell us something about the importance of reviewing and evaluating? You bet.

We Can Do Tuesday Films

How does all this apply to us?

VALUABLE LESSON	
#29	Evaluating what works and doesn't work in business is essential to developing conscious competence.

When I trained for that first marathon, I measured my progress on a weekly basis. How many miles had I run? How many days had I run that week? What stopped me when I did not run? What made it easier or harder?

This process of reviewing and evaluating and adjusting brought me closer to my goal of 26.2 miles.

Evaluating what works and doesn't work in business is essential to developing conscious competence. Each day, take at least a few minutes to review. What activities were you committed to that day, and how close did you come to accomplishing them? Did the activities further your mission? How close are you to reaching the weekly or monthly goals you have set? What worked or did not work? What distracted you?

Defining your results today allows you to adjust your actions tomorrow and become more efficient and effective. Consciously competent people are the big winners. They power up and go for it! They are the ones who can truly relish their achievements. And they will surely end up in their own Hall of Fame.

PART 3: THE CLOCK

"You'd better be early. If you're on time, you're late."
  –Tom Coughlin, NFL Coach

Chapter 22

MAKE THE CLOCK YOUR FRIEND (OR AT LEAST DON'T LET IT BE YOUR ENEMY!)

"Time is life. It is irreversible and irreplaceable. To waste your time is to waste your life. But to master your time is to master your life and make the most of it."
    –Alan Lakein

This is my favorite quote and one I live by. It is from the book *How to Get Control of Your Time and Your Life* by Lakein, a time management guru. He also wrote another one of my favorite sayings: *"Failing to plan is planning to fail."*

Managing time is a challenge for everyone. Some people are better at it than others. Some people are good at it, even though they don't

> Managing time is a challenge for everyone.

like doing it, because they know it's a critical part of success. Whether you're a natural at time management or not, you can realize rewards from the lessons that football provides about managing time.

Control the Clock

In football, it's called Clock Management, because the play clock during a game continues to run between most plays. They even say "controlling the clock" which I love. A team that's behind will eventually discover that the clock is their enemy. Time will simply run out for them. So, the coach needs to be able to "control the clock" if he expects his team to win.

The coach is tasked with overall clock management. He needs to be very aware of how much time is left in the game, how many time-outs his team has left, what part of the field his team is on, and what kind of plays to call. It's amazing to watch a master of clock management guide his team to a victory that only moments ago looked impossible. It's an inspiring thing to witness.

The quarterback also needs to be able to control the clock. His focus stays on the field, making sure all the players have the right play in mind, they're at the line of scrimmage, and the right substitutions have been made.

Are You Formal or Casual?

When it comes to us, it's more subtle. People have different styles with time. Some people are formal with time; you know who you are. You're usually fairly organized. You have a schedule, and a To Do list. And you are always very early! If you're five minutes early, you are late. You need to be twenty minutes early.

You know you are formal with time if you spend a certain amount of time per day in an activity called "Waiting!" Waiting for people. Waiting for things to begin. It's a minor annoyance, but somehow we formal people don't seem to mind. In fact, we are always early in order to avoid the heart-thumping nervousness we feel when we entertain the notion of being "just on time." And of course we have things to do while we wait: things to read and calls to make. We make good use of waiting.

Other people have a casual relationship with time. They are thrilled when they are not late. They congratulate themselves when they are "just on time." These are usually the same people who don't mind missing the beginning of a movie, TV show, or play. This drives the formal people crazy! One casual friend said, "I don't know why you're upset. This is the earliest I've ever been late."

The problem comes when a formal person is early to a meeting, and the casual person breezes in and sits down next to the formal person just as the meeting is about to begin. The formal person turns to the casual person and makes the classic passive-aggressive verbal sound of disapproval, which goes like this: "Tsk, sigh." The casual person gets defensive and says, "What is your problem?" The formal person may say something like, "You don't respect my time." The casual person rolls his eyes and says "You need to chill."

This conflict comes into sharper focus when you marry or live with or work closely with a person of the opposite style. For instance, when you go on a romantic vacation together, the formal person wants to leave waaaaaayyyyy earlier than the casual person. The formal person doesn't mind getting to the airport in advance of the scheduled departure because they have things to do while they are waiting — productive things, fun things, satisfying things.

The casual person thinks waiting at the airport is a stupid waste of time. Their perfect scenario is to walk up to the gate as the plane is boarding and sashay straight onto the jetway. This strikes fear into the heart of the formal person. "We might miss the flight!" "I like a moment to find my seat, get settled and relax!" "There won't be any room in the overhead!"

We formal people who are so righteous, let me tell you something: casual people have a much more relaxed life than we do because we are the designated worriers. On the way to the airport, we have impending disaster scenarios in our heads such as, "What if there's traffic?" "What if the car breaks down?" "What if the freeway is… gone?" This is why we leave early enough so that if all those things happened, we would still be early! Casual people feel our angst. If you have ever been accused of "filling the car with bad vibes," you are a formal person.

Tom Coughlin: Formal Guy

Tom Coughlin, coach of the Super Bowl-winning New York Giants, is a very formal person with time. When he became head coach in 2004, he demanded his players be early to their meetings. For one such meeting, Michael Strahan, a star defensive end, was only FIVE minutes early and was fined by Coughlin for not being early

> Nothing shuts up complainers like winning.

ENOUGH. Strahan went on several sports shows complaining. But then they started winning games. And the complaining stopped. Nothing shuts up complainers like winning. And when the Giants went on to win the Super Bowl, I have to admit, it warmed the cockles of my very-formal-with-time heart.

Solution for Your Romantic Vacation

By the way, I have a most elegant solution for the airport dilemma. Ready? Go to the airport separately and meet at the gate! One takes the car; the other takes a cab. Engineer it so both travelers get their preferred way.

This system sometimes results in the casual person missing the plane. So be it!

When Mr. Casual arrives at the hotel, he finds Ms. Formal soaking in a luxurious bubble bath. No nagging. No finger-pointing. No bad vibes. She has started without him. This way, they don't spend the first two days of their romantic (and expensive) vacation arguing about "We almost missed the plane!" versus "We made the plane!"

Know If They Are Formal or Casual

VALUABLE LESSON	
#30	In business, knowing who is formal with time and who is casual can be very valuable.

In business, knowing who is formal with time and who is casual can be very valuable. If you have not already guessed, I am formal. I am always 20 minutes early to an appointment. As I approach the receptionist, I can tell if her boss is formal or casual by the look on her face.

If she looks panicked, I know the boss is casual, and not ready for me. I quickly put her at ease, saying, "I'm early. Not to worry. I have things to do." She looks relieved and says, "Oh, good. She's not ready for you."

If, on the other hand, I walk up to a receptionist who looks excited,

VALUABLE LESSON	
#31	When your time is your own, do whatever you want. When someone else is involved, especially in business where money is also involved, learn to control the clock.

I know the boss is formal. The receptionist will say, "Mimi Donaldson? You're early." (Please note the self-satisfied smile on my face right about now), "I will tell him you're here." I know I have just given her a gift: a happy boss who can now run ahead of schedule.

When your time is your own, do whatever you want. When someone else is involved, especially in business where money is also involved, learn to control the clock.

Worked for the Giants!

CHAPTER 23

TIME OF POSSESSION: DON'T DROP THE BALL

"Our mentality is we play 2-minute offense the whole game. There has to be a sense of urgency."
–Peyton Manning

One particularly fearsome defensive player was once asked why he was so tenacious on the field, why he was so aggressive, why he tackled so hard. His answer was most profound. He said, "If we don't have the ball, we can't score."

This is true. Very true. So true in its simplicity, it's genius. If you don't have the ball, you can't score. So, your defense has to stop the other team from having the ball. And the best way to do that

VALUABLE LESSON	
#32	If you don't have the ball, you can't score.

is to be a particularly fearsome defensive player.

This is called time of possession. Time of possession is extremely important. Unless your team has possession of the ball, meaning your offense is on the field, you cannot succeed, you cannot achieve the goal. The team who wins usually had possession of the ball longer. In a 60-minute football game, the winning team's time of possession is typically about 40 minutes versus the losing team's 20 or so minutes of possession. So get the ball.

Manning Breaks Tradition

There are no points for having the ball longer. And sometimes the team with less time of possession wins the game. But rarely. Unless Peyton Manning is your quarterback. In week 2 of the '09 season, he led the Colts to a victory with the lowest time of possession since 1977. The Colts had the ball 14 minutes and 53 seconds. Their opponent, the Miami Dolphins had the ball for 45 minutes and 7 seconds. At the press conference after the game, Manning said, "It's being efficient; it's what the game is all about."

Take the Ball

Same is true in life. We need to be efficient with our time AND have possession.

Having possession of the ball in life means taking responsibility. The more time you spend being responsible, the more points you will score.

> In life, we need to be efficient with our time AND have possession.

It's as simple as that. Accept responsibility: for your work, your actions, for everything you do and say. When you are in a meeting, sit in the front row. When the manager asks for volunteers, raise your hand.

Embrace responsibility. Make it a habit. Spend less time pointing fingers and blaming others. That's a waste of your time and energy. Reinvest that time and energy in pursuit of your goals, figuring out solutions to problems, and overcoming obstacles.

We all know people who seem to breeze through the day without contributing to their department's productivity. Sometimes, they even get some of the credit. When we do make a major contribution, sometimes it may not get recognized to the extent we feel we deserve. Sometimes, we chalk this up to "too bad," and get over it. Sometimes, we take note and communicate it to the boss. We need to toot our horns a bit more.

In football, there is a lot of "get over it" and that's okay with most players. They understand the inherent fairness and unfairness of the game. And they go about their business accordingly.

The more you accept life's responsibilities and the longer you spend working toward your goals, the better off you will be. See? It's all about time of possession!

VALUABLE LESSON	
#33	The more you accept life's responsibilities and the longer you spend working toward your goals, the better off you will be. See? It's all about time of possession!

CHAPTER 24

TIME OUT: BLOWING YOUR INTERNAL WHISTLE

"The two most powerful warriors are patience and time."
–Leo Tolstoy

On the football field, everything does not always go smoothly. When the offensive team is disorganized on the field, the defense amps up their energy because they can sense a big play coming. Often the next offensive play is a fumble or interception or some other mishap caused as much by the defense as by the offense. A team in disarray on the field will often screw up. In this situation, an experienced quarterback will call a time-out. It lets his players catch their breath, center their thoughts, get a drink of water, walk off the aches. It allows the quarterback and coaches a moment to devise a winning play.

VALUABLE LESSON	
#34	A time-out allows the quarterback and coaches a moment to devise a winning play.

Put Your Game on "Pause"

It's like putting the game on "pause" for a moment. This pause is your internal whistle. Remember, when the whistle blows the play is over. It's a good idea to be aware of your internal whistle in life and have it ready everywhere you go. And you don't always need a 30-second time-out, like in football. Sometimes, all you need is a momentary break to get your act together.

VALUABLE LESSON	
#35	It's a good idea to be aware of your internal whistle in life and have it ready everywhere you go.

Of course, sometimes we forget we have an internal whistle, especially when someone else is pushing *our* hot buttons. For example, you ask a co-worker to do something and she responds, "That's not my job." Feeling your blood pressure rise, you may be tempted to blurt out, "Well, it's not mine either, Knucklehead!"

This response may come to your mind, but it needn't come out of your mouth. Remember: You have the internal whistle. You realize if you utter your response, you won't get the job done and you will alienate the co-worker. (Friends come and go; enemies accumulate.)

Friends come and go; enemies accumulate.

So, instead you say, "I understand." And you do. The person feels overworked and underpaid. (Don't we all?) Then you may say, "I know you're swamped, but this thing has to get done to meet the deadline. Can you give it any time at all?" And understanding begins. Now you have a chance of actually getting what you want.

Don't Retaliate

In football, 95% of the penalties are called on the player who retaliates — not instigates — the unnecessary roughness or unsportsmanlike conduct. It's like a mom who sees one of her kids hit his brother or sister. No amount of "but she started it" will dissuade Mom. She often punishes both. The referee throws the flag on the retaliator, so blow your internal whistle.

We've seen how blowing your internal whistle gives us an opportunity to stop, reassess, and improve our performance. The results are usually better than if we had kept on going, panicking the whole time, throwing crazy passes, scrambling around hysterically.

VALUABLE LESSON	
#36	The referee throws the flag on the retaliator, so blow your internal whistle.

But what happens when it's late in the game, when it gets down to crunch time and we still haven't scored? Is it time to give up? Throw in the towel? Forfeit?

No!

There is another pause strategy in football that can work for us. It's called killing the clock. Already it has a satisfying ring to it, doesn't it? Killing the clock. There are times in life when we'd all like to kill the clock. And football, once again, serves up the perfect parallel.

In the waning seconds of a game, behind by only a few points, with

VALUABLE LESSON	
#37	Don't be afraid to kill the clock. Many a victory has been snatched from the jaws of defeat with the effective use of killing the clock.

time running out, sometimes it's necessary to waste a play and kill the clock. To understand this, you first have to know that in football, whenever a quarterback throws a pass and it isn't caught, the clock stops until the next play starts. The quarterback can

spike — throw the football into the ground — for an intentional incomplete pass.

The downside is it counts as a play. So, you have one less opportunity (or "down") to run another play. But the upside is, with the clock stopped, you can huddle up, call a brilliant play, line up, and pull off a game-winner. In your life, don't be afraid to kill the clock. This is not a race to the finish. You have some control.

Killing the clock is a stop-gap measure. You are in emergency mode. But many a victory has been snatched from the jaws of defeat with the effective use of killing the clock. It allows your team at least one more chance at a reasoned, considered play.

And if that doesn't work, you've always got the Hail Mary.

CHAPTER 25

TWO-MINUTE DRILL: WHEN THE GAME IS ON THE LINE

*"Most games are won in the last two minutes of the first half
or at the end of the second half."*
    –Vince Lombardi

When the legendary football coach Vince Lombardi uttered the quote above, his point was this: Don't lose your focus just as you're about to achieve your goal — the game-winning touchdown. Even a field goal can win the game, and no one knew that better than Lombardi. Field goal kickers are rarely anyone's favorite player (unless they can get you tickets), but they are a great example of nailing a victory in the waning seconds of a game. Actually, field goal kickers are the highest scoring players on a team, and you'd be surprised how often a win comes down to the field goal. The kicker can make the difference between winning and losing. They are the unsung heroes of the game.

Why Two Minutes?

Two minutes has emerged as a natural length of time to make a game-winning score. In every football game, each half has an automatic two-minute time-out and this is called when the clock reaches the last two minutes. Then, in the last two minutes of actual play, they run a "hurry up offense" with no huddle time and quick snaps from the quarterback to use the time efficiently. Every team has its own special version or versions of the two-minute drill.

Here's how it works, and maybe you'll get a sense of how closely the two-minute drill relates to life. The average two-minute drill means your team needs to cover roughly 90 yards in 120 seconds while eleven guys on the opposing team are trying to stop you from doing that. I'm sure you'll agree this is no small task. But once your team establishes "forward motion," you strive to keep it alive. Second chances are hard to come by, particularly at the end of a game.

A Sense of Urgency

Being in the two-minute drill intensifies the situational pressure as you can well imagine. The good news is that the sense of urgency creates additional energy, too. If you can tap into this extra reserve of energy, and channel it toward your desired outcome, the pressure becomes an ally rather than an enemy.

VALUABLE LESSON	
#38	The sense of urgency creates additional energy, too. If you can tap into this extra reserve of energy, and channel it toward your desired outcome, the pressure becomes an ally rather than an enemy.

By turning situational stress into an advantage, you can spend some of your newly found resources on becoming acutely aware of your surroundings. For football players it means scanning the horizon for potential problems. When linebackers want to take your head off, make last-second adjustments based on what the opposing team is doing, and initiate your plan on the spot.

The focus of the team shifts. Teams practice two-minute drills over and over again so the routine is wired in and ready when it's needed. When you only have two minutes to score there isn't a whole lot of time for improvisation. In other words, you have to create your own opportunities. This is where conditioning and preparation come in. Obviously, football players have to be in great physical shape, and that's not a bad idea for everyday people, too. But the kind of conditioning and preparation demanded in the non-football world is more mental.

> The first part of any successful plan is to remember what you did right the last time you were in a similar situation.

In football, when a player makes a boneheaded play, the coach will yell, "Get your head in the game!" This is excellent advice. Shake off the mental haze clouding your head and concentrate on your objective. It always helps to have a plan.

The first part of any successful plan is to remember what you did right the last time you were in a similar situation. Keep those strategies and tactics at your fingertips because they will very likely come in handy again. It's always useful to be a student of the game. Outside of football we call it being a lifelong learner. Having a healthy historical perspective on what has worked and what hasn't makes for a solid foundation in formulating a good plan.

Once a coach has mapped out a rough plan for his team, it's up to the individual players to execute that plan. Oddly enough, good plans can fail because of inferior execution while bad plans can succeed with superior execution. The most important factors in effective execution are laser focus, complete concentration, a competitive spirit, stepping it up, and never saying die.

Laser Focus

Develop the ability to sharpen your focus on the task at hand. No goofing off. Center your thoughts on the exact picture of what you want to achieve. An offensive lineman, charged with the task of protecting his quarterback, will analyze the stance of the opposing player he must stop, making a note of approximately where his opponent's center of gravity is. Then, as the play begins, the lineman will mentally "zoom in" on that area of the opposing player's body, attacking that spot, pushing through that critical location, landing him on his back while the quarterback, unfettered, throws a touchdown pass. That's focus.

Being in the game, on the field, forces you to focus on the situation at hand. You can't ignore it. If you do, it'll flatten you. In the everyday world, you only have your mission and your ambition to make you focus.

VALUABLE LESSON	
#39	Develop the ability to sharpen your focus on the task at hand.

Complete Concentration

This is very similar to laser focus, except it's all mental. Yogi Berra once said, "90% of the game is half mental." With due deference to Yogi's math skills, he's about right. In Kevin Costner's baseball movie, *For Love of the Game,* before each pitch, he would force his mind to "clear the machine." He removed external distractions from his brain as he began his windup. In the movie, his concentration

VALUABLE LESSON	
#40	In the everyday world, you only have your mission and your ambition to make you focus.

was depicted by the crowd suddenly going silent. It was very powerful. There was no goofing off, just total concentration.

Competitive Spirit

Having a competitive spirit makes achieving success more likely. If a big guy wants to knock you down, wrap your mind around one simple concept: Knock him down instead (not literally, of course). Harder. Faster. One short burst of targeted energy and it's over. You've won.

Sometimes, you are your biggest competitor. Believe in yourself and learn to get out of your own way. Get rid of that defeatist attitude so you can overcome other difficulties. Otherwise you've made the job just that much harder. As you begin exploring your inner competitive spirit, remember that in the midst of the two-minute drill, glory is short lived. In life, just like in football, you have to pick yourself up, brush yourself off, jog back to the huddle, and await your next assignment. It's simple but not easy. But it's what the game calls for. It's what life calls for, too. Answer the call. Answer it now. You'll be duly rewarded.

VALUABLE LESSON	
#41	Believe in yourself and learn to get out of your own way.

Stepping It Up

The two-minute drill will come in handy in many aspects of your life. For example, once you've built up a little bit of momentum, use that energy to keep your game plan rolling. Add to it. Push a little harder. Move a little faster. Maintain a clear view of your goals.

The whole idea of the two-minute drill is that victory can be had with one more successful score. The game is on the line. You can win or lose, depending on what you make happen.

> You win or lose, depending on what you make happen.

When you're watching a game, and the score is 20–15, the announcer will often say something like this: "The Colts are within five points, and a touchdown will win the game. It's almost like we're at the very beginning of the game!" Herein lies a small truth about human nature. Even though these players have been slugging it out, play after play, for nearly three hours, they can gain a new fresh perspective on the situation if they take a brand new look at it. Never mind the past. It's left the building. How you got here isn't important. How hard you've worked isn't important. How tired you are isn't important. Start fresh. Approach those last two minutes, just as you would if the score were 0–0 with a full 60 minutes to play. You might find that you can actually accomplish your goal with hardly any time remaining on the clock, just because you decided to take a new and fresh approach.

Never Say Die

Are you a good two-minute drill player? Let's say that in your working life you have a list of six calls you need to get done before lunch. It's almost lunchtime, and you've done four calls, and they all went poorly. They weren't dismal failures, but neither were they glowing successes. The other team didn't score, but you put no points on the board either. Call your next play. What is it? Punt? Quit? Give up? Fumble? Head for the locker room? Why bother? LUNCHTIME!

Or do you gather your thoughts and lock in on your task, tighten your chinstrap, put your head down, and start driving forward with a sufficient amount of energy to get the job done? Do you look for any available opening and exploit any opportunity to further your cause?

You can do it. It's more a matter of will than of ability. And the ironic thing is that you have more control over your will than you do over your ability. Ability is a gift. Will is your choice.

So… be determined!

Facing the two-minute drill can be viewed as a problem or an opportunity. It's your choice. Choose wisely.

Do yourself a favor and approach the closing moments of any contest as methodically as possible: One Play At A Time. Don't think about the next play until it's time. Don't think about the last play… AT ALL! If you can train yourself to do this, Vince Lombardi would be proud.

You'll face a lot of two-minute drills in your life. The momentary pressure will make many demands on you. But if you rise to the occasion, you will be presented with the ideal opportunity to claim victory. If you avoid being sucked into the vortex of indecision or insecurity, the two-minute drill can become your moment to shine.

VALUABLE LESSON

#42 Ability is a gift. Will is your choice.

Yes, it's tough. So what? Figure it out and practice over and over and over again. Marines have a saying: "Improvise. Adapt. Overcome." Not only is this great advice, even the order in which words appear is important. That's the code of the two-minute drill, and the best part is that you can do it. Why do I say this? Because football players already have, again and again and again. Don't let the clock run out on you; give it your best shot and chances are you'll come out a winner.

PART 4: POST GAME

Men and Women: Can We Talk?

I've been making audiences laugh for years with tales of differences between men and women, and I've learned many valuable insights about men from football.

I say men compartmentalize and live in "blocks;" women connect everything together and live in "flow."

Recently, I watched the old movie, *The Grapes of Wrath*, with a young Henry Fonda. In the last scene, Henry Fonda's Ma, played by Jane Darwell, intones the following speech to Pa:

"A woman can change better than a man. A man lives, well, sort of, in jerks. A baby's born, and somebody dies, and that's a jerk. He gets a farm, and loses it, and that's a jerk.

With a woman, it's all in one flow, like a stream — the eddies and waterfalls — but the river, it goes right on. A woman looks at it that way."

Jane Darwell won an Oscar for her performance. This was in 1940. Is there nothing new under the sun? The following chapters illuminate the differences between males and females, and bridge the gender gap in communication. Goal? A happier life!

CHAPTER 26

DON'T TELL ME A STORY: GIMME THE BOTTOM LINE

"Football is a man's game. All that is flawed and
uncontrollable and beautiful about men is there in it...
Football speaks to something basic within the male system, to
the testosterone and dark cave principles, that drip through
the crania and loins of our half of the species."
  –Rick Telander, from his book, Like a Rose.

On the field and off, men don't use a lot of words. One guy turns to another and says, "Lunch?" The other guy says, "Sure."

That's it.

They don't say, "Wanna go to lunch?" "Yeah, it sounds like a great idea." "Where shall we go?" "I don't know, where shall we go?" And so on.

No.

"Lunch?" The other guy says, "Sure." Done deal.

Girls Use More Words

This pattern starts in childhood. My friend has a boy and a girl. They returned from their first day of school. My friend asked each of them how the first day of school went. The little boy said, "Fine. Can I go play ball?" The little girl said, "Well, I got on the bus and there was Suzy. So I sat next to her and...and then... and then..." She took 15 minutes to answer the question.

The children were each communicating in their own gender-based style. This style comes naturally. Studies show that women use an average of 25,000 words in a typical day. Men use about 15,000. I always quip, "The problem is by the time men come home from work, they've used all 15,000 up. We haven't even started on our 25,000. We've had to be concise all day long!"

My old boyfriend used to hang on every word of my stories. Then we got serious. I started a story, and he stopped me, saying, "Meem, wait. Are you going to do, 'He said, she said, he said, she said?'" That was his code for the way I tell stories from the beginning with the details, chronologically to the end. (Men are wincing just reading this.)

VALUABLE LESSON	
#43	Men seem to be more about the destination than the journey. Women are all about the journey.

And I remember my response, "Tsk (sigh)." Men hate that response because it's a sneaky, non-assertive, passive-aggressive way of saying, "You stupid idiot," without actually saying it.

I said, in a disparaging tone, "Tsk (sigh). Yes, Honey. That's how the story is enjoyed the best."

And he said, "Not by me. Can you just skip to the bottom line?"

I remember feeling offended. I thought he was going to miss the good part. Then I discovered the story is not the good part for him. He really did want the bottom line. Men seem to be more about the destination than the journey. Women are all about the journey.

When I put a moratorium on my storytelling, my boyfriend had to *beg* me to tell him the whole story. And he had to promise to listen *all* the way through, without the hand-rolling gesture. Women hate that gesture because it's a sneaky, non-assertive, passive-aggressive way of saying, "Hurry up!" without actually saying it. It's the male version of "Tsk (sigh)" and if they use it too often, I know plenty of women who will use an alternate hand gesture.

Men Want the Bottom Line

In football, it's the same. Men just want to get to the goal. That's the only thing that matters to them.

In football, when a player on the field fumbles the ball, it's up for grabs. Anyone on either side can recover it. If the opposing team gets it, their offense comes on the field and starts trying to score by reaching their goal line. Change of possession. Here's how I know men are only interested in the bottom line. When a ball carrier coughs up the ball, all the players on both teams start yelling, "Ball! Ball! Ball!" That means only one thing to a player: "Stop what you're doing and start looking for the ball. It's up for grabs! Get it!!!" No one says something like, "Oh, my goodness. The ball has been fumbled. Please look around for it. It must be around here somewhere."

> "Tsk (sigh)." Men hate that response because it's a sneaky, non-assertive, passive-aggressive way of saying, "You stupid idiot," without actually saying it.

No. Men have shortened it to one word. Ball! Because that's the bottom line.

Some men just "get" it. My friend, Dan Moriarty interviewed me on FOX Sports Radio before this book was finished. He is the best interviewer I have ever heard, because he really LISTENS. Dan spent twelve years on TV and the past seven simultaneously on the radio. Huge celebrities routinely tell him, "I have never said this before," as they reveal themselves. Dan says this skill comes naturally and is inspired by his outstanding relationship with his wife and two daughters. Dan is an ex-hockey player, and in my opinion it does not get more macho than that. But he is at the forefront of great male-to-female relationships. Dan leads the way with a style of interviewing to which both men and women can relate.

CHAPTER 27

PLAYING WITHOUT A PLAYBOOK

*"Remember, men and women communicate differently.
That's the beginning of communication; understanding
and agreement are rules of engagement."*
–Lula Bailey Ballton, from her book,
50 Saturdays Before You Say 'I Do'.

Going to Lunch

Women relax and socialize differently than men. Often, women do not have a plan. Men typically have a plan, like the 150 plays on the wristband of the quarterback. Let's use the same example from the previous chapter to illustrate the difference: Going to Lunch.

For years, in my training classrooms, I have been excusing people to go to lunch. They usually have about an hour. When women go to lunch together, they drift to the bathroom, talking all the way. Subjects ebb and flow, every subject except lunch. A woman thinks since she is already going to lunch, it frees her to talk

> A woman thinks since she is already going to lunch, it frees her to talk about other things.

about other things. Women form natural clusters in the bathroom, in the lobby, in the parking lot. Eventually, one woman says, "Where are we going?"

"We don't know. We don't care," reply the other women. They are already having a great time. Lunch has begun.

But practical matters intrude, such as who's going to drive. No one wants to drive a group of women who don't know nor care where they're going. The driver knows she will be in charge and won't be free to have as much fun as the others. Finally, someone says reluctantly, "Okay, I'll drive (tsk… sigh); my car is closest." She's not happy. First of all, she needs to clean out her car. Women nest in their cars. We travel with food, water, office supplies, parking meter coins, magazines, towels, even a change of clothes. How many of us have running shoes in the trunk in case we are stranded somewhere in high heels?

Back to the lunch. The women are all in the car, talking of course, and having a wonderful time. Except the driver. "Ladies?" the driver asks. "Where are we going?"

No one answers; they are having too good a time. "We don't know. We don't care. Just go," someone says and she makes the Universal Hand Gesture of pushing forward with the back of her hand.

"All right, Ladies, I'm pulling out of the parking lot. Which way shall I turn?" The driver is lonely. She wants some help. She wants the others to share her pain.

No one pays any attention; they are having too much fun. Finally someone says, "Turn right." Why? It's the easiest way to turn. Sometimes, someone will say, "Go left." If there is a man in the car, he will ask, "Why?" And she will give him a female answer: "It feels like there will be restaurants that way. It looks like the kind of street restaurants will be on." I have never heard a man say this.

Then the man in the car will ask the four-word man question, "How do you know?" Men want to trust your way of knowing. Women sometimes give men the most frustrating answer: "I don't know *how* I know. I just know."

Again, back to the lunch. What if there are no restaurants that way? Women just turn around and go the other way. There's no man in the car saying, "See?"

Women find a restaurant just as scientifically. Someone points to one, and says, "Look! Let's go there. That one looks... cute."

"We're going there," the driver says. She can't wait to stop driving, so she can start having fun with everyone else. They all tromp to the door, and here's a real difference between men and women. The sign on the door says, "Closed Monday" and it's Monday. What do women do? "Awww," they say. "Wouldn't you know it?" And they pile back into the car to find another restaurant.

Men, on the other hand, have decided on the restaurant in advance, appointed the driver, and have their taste buds up for what they are going to order. If men tromp up to the door, and the sign says, "Closed Monday," male reactions range from, "Who picked this place?" to mild rage, accompanied by impugning the chooser's manhood and other insults. I know ex-military, aerospace engineers who cannot take it when the restaurant they picked is closed.

> The four-word man question, "How do you know?" Men want to trust your way of knowing.

It jams their systems. These are the same guys who will never ask for directions when they're lost. I am sure that's why Moses wandered 40 years in the desert; he would not ask for directions.

"Finding" A Restaurant

Here's another example of male/female difference.

On a first dinner date, a fellow asked me to choose a restaurant in my neighborhood. When he came to pick me up, he asked, "Do you know how to get there?" I said, "Sure, I've been there before." I meant I could "find" my way there. He did not mean that at all. When we reached a large, busy intersection, he asked, "Do we turn right or left?"

"I'm not sure," I replied. Using the same Universal Hand Gesture of pushing forward with the back of my hand, I asked, "Can you pull up a little so I can look?" I will never forget the look he gave me; I knew I had broken some unspoken rule of men and directions.

VALUABLE LESSON	
#44	The point of all this is: when you're with a man, even if it's four women and just one hapless guy, have a plan. Just like in football, when they call a play in the huddle, they have a plan.

The guy behind us honked, and my date was not happy, to say the least. I had caused him to lose face in front of another guy when he had to pull up a little and then stop again.

There was no second date.

But I got a great story for my speech and this book.

The point of all this is: when you're with a man, even if it's four women and just one hapless guy, have a plan. Just like in football, when they call a play in the huddle, they have a plan.

Or, better yet, make everyone happy. Let the women have their wonderful time while letting the man fulfill his destiny; make HIM drive!

CHAPTER  28

THE MUTE BUTTON AND OTHER MALE FANTASIES

"Women marry men hoping they will change. Men
marry women hoping they will not. So each is inevitably
disappointed."
  –Albert Einstein

Watch ESPN

"You never listen to me!" Ever hear a woman say this? Ever say it yourself? The way around it is to use the ESPN model. I learned more about communicating with men from the shows on ESPN than I ever learned in any communication courses. If you want to have men listen to you, watch *Sports Center, Pardon the Interruption or Around the Horn.* These shows will show you how men prefer to receive information.

On the screen there is a list of the topics as they are coming up. The topic is highlighted as it's being talked about. The idea can be illustrated best by employing *The Three Tells*.

1. Tell them what you're going to tell them.
2. Tell them.
3. Tell them what you just told them.

(By the way, you learned this in 8th grade speech class!)

Number 1 gets them excited because they know what's going to happen next. They love this. They get to look forward to something, even if it's going to happen right away. Men like to be prepared. In football, they need to know the play.

Number 2 is the actual information. Since they've been prepared by Number 1, they get to be right. Again, they love this.

> Men especially love getting to say, "I knew that."

Number 3 gives them a chance to say "Yup-I knew it," because THEY DID! You just told them. So they already know this, even if it's only been 11 seconds. Men especially love getting to say, "I knew that." *The Three Tells* is a concept that I'm sure was written by a man. And even if it wasn't, at least ESPN knows to use it in their broadcasts.

How to Avoid Being Muted

Men always want to know, "How long will it take?" And ESPN knows that, too. On most shows, there is a timer on the screen. You can watch the seconds tick down as the panelists discuss each topic. Again, men love knowing how much time is elapsing. Even when they're looking forward to the thing that happens, they still want to know how long it will be.

On ESPN's *Around the Horn*, they go a step further and make a game of it! They call it "the show that scores the argument." The host arbitrarily awards points to or deducts points from each commentator. And beyond that, if the host really doesn't like what he hears, he gets to use the Ultimate Male Fantasy: the MUTE button!

> Most men can shift into "Selective Listening" mode, their built-in MUTE button.

Most men have this power naturally; it's part of their DNA.

When they start hearing stuff they don't want to hear, they can shift into "Selective Listening" mode. This is their built-in MUTE button. You may still be talking, but they are no longer actively listening.

I have a friend who tests her husband whenever she suspects he has tuned out. She'll start to add phrases like: "And then I sold the kids to some gypsies," or "And then the house caught fire and burned to the ground," or "And then I ran around the front yard naked until the neighbors called the cops!" Usually he quickly realizes he has pushed his internal Mute Button on her. But every now and then she gets the pre-programmed response of: "That's nice, dear." Busted!

VALUABLE LESSON	
#45	For men, talk is the simple exchange of information. For women, talk is bonding.

If you want to avoid being "muted," do what the sports shows do: learn the value of *The Three Tells*. Because for men, talk is the simple exchange of information. For women, talk is bonding.

Men and Women Bond Differently

Men bond through competitive mind games. They test each other with questions. "Who won the Super Bowl in 1984?" If the other guy knows, he gets a point. And if he doesn't, that's fine, too, because the first guy is one up. And the other guy will have to get him back. That's how men bond. It's a good system. It's just not the way women do it.

Women don't bond through test questions. In fact, if a woman asks another woman who won the Super Bowl in 1984, the listener may extend both arms and say, "Do you need a hug?" And she probably would. Because that behavior isn't normal. Women don't bond through competition.

Men bond through competitive mind games.

Women bond through stories. You walk up to a woman you hardly know. You say, "Gee, I love that necklace. It's beautiful." And she says, "Thank you," and proceeds to tell you The Story Behind The Necklace. Because... *there is one!* Women have a story for every piece of clothing and jewelry on their bodies. They have a story for their haircut. Some of us have stories about our hair color or colors.

The bonding starts to happen when the listener finds something in her story she can relate to, and then tells her a story back. If you have enough stories in common, you will bond. It takes a little longer than the Super Bowl trivia questions, but it works just as well.

Women bond through stories.

How Long Will This Take?

Another one of the beauties of the game of football is: it only lasts a certain amount of time. Men like this. At the end, the team with the most points wins! It's that simple. Unless the score is tied — then the game goes into overtime. But even then, the players can gear up for it because they've seen it coming.

Even on the practice field, players are told how long each training exercise will last. They get a schedule in advance. It looks like this and they love it!

08:50AM–10:10AM: General Practice and Proper Running Mechanics

10:20AM–11:40AM: Speed, Agility, Quickness, Balance and Core Strength Workout

11:50AM–12:10PM: Cool Down and Therapy

12:30PM–01:30PM: LUNCH!

01:50PM–02:30PM: Position-Specific Strength Training: Power and Endurance

02:40PM–04:00PM: **Squad Scrimmages**

04:10PM–04:40PM: **Flexibility Training and Acceleration Techniques**

It's a Matter of Energy

Why do they love it? Because all men want to know how long things will take. They don't like surprises. They feel responsible for allotting energy to a certain activity. Men don't want to run out.

Women don't even think about this. They don't know where their energy comes from. It just comes. They get it from talking and shopping; they get second winds and third winds. And they don't think about running out. In fact, when a women runs out of energy, she calls a female buddy to share the event. She says, "You are not going to believe this. I am *totally* out of energy! I'm surprised I had enough energy to dial the phone!" You can hear pleasure and relish in her voice. It is almost sensual. The other woman enjoys this. She says, "I cannot believe it. You? Out of energy? Amazing!"

> **VALUABLE LESSON**
>
> **#46** When a man asks how long will it take, don't assume he doesn't want to do it

Can you imagine a guy calling up another guy and saying, "Hey. I'm really tired." Never! That would be a loss of face. The only person to whom a man is willing to admit that to is the person he loves. And that's how you know he loves you.

So, when a man asks how long will it take, don't assume he doesn't want to do it. He's not being clever. He's not hinting that he would rather not. He simply and honestly wants to know how much energy he needs to dedicate to the forthcoming task or activity so he won't run out. So tell him!

Want to go a step further? When you want to really endear yourself to a man, tell him a conversation is going to take 20 minutes, then take 15 minutes. Tell him this activity will take 30 minutes, then take 20. It is like coming in ahead of schedule and under budget! It builds trust.

It's like a football player getting to skip Flexibility Training and Acceleration Techniques. What player isn't going to appreciate that?

CHAPTER 29

HINTING: IT'S NOT ROMANTIC!

*"Don't keep a man guessing too long — he's sure to find the
answer somewhere else."*
  –Mae West

No Subtleties Here

In football there aren't a lot of subtleties. It's mostly about the obvious. It's mostly about the biggest, the fastest, the strongest, and the best. Not that the game is without its strategic details, that's what makes it fascinating on so many levels. But mostly, it's about 11 men wanting to move in one direction while 11 other men want to stop them from doing that. Basic. Obvious. Not subtle.

Women can learn an important insight into men. Men are not subtle. Nor do they value mind reading. No hints, ladies! Just come right out and say it. If you want to make certain that a man fully understands what's on your mind, SAY

VALUABLE LESSON	
#47	If you want to make certain that a man fully understands what's on your mind, SAY IT.

IT. This technique applies to men who work for you, men you work for, and men in your house.

Typical example: A woman (me — this is my story) will give a man big hints over and over, such as, "I love flowers." And no flowers ever arrive. So, she gives him *huge* hints over and over; when she sees a person give another person flowers, she says to him, "Oh look. I love flowers." More waiting, more no flowers.

Finally, she decides to be direct. "Honey," she says one day, "do you know what I would really love you to do?"

He looks up attentively. That is a focusing statement. It gives him hope that the next thing out of her mouth will be specific. Men love this. "What?" he asks.

She loves this: 100% attention on his part. She says, "I would love you to bring me flowers sometime when I least expect it, like on my birthday."

> **VALUABLE LESSON**
>
> **#48** Men usually say what they mean and mean what they say. The trouble arises when they expect women to do the same.

It registers. He gets the message. She can tell it clicks. She gets gorgeous flowers on her birthday. She is so happy. Her women friends are livid. "You had to tell him," they say. "It's not romantic. He should have known," they say.

"Yeah, right," she shoots back. "On the one hand, I could have, 'He should have known.' On the other hand, I could have FLOWERS." So she went for the flowers. And she was so glad she did.

Men are Literal

Later, when she debriefs him on this incident, she may say, "What were you thinking when I said I loved flowers?" Again, he loves this question; it's analytical. He says, "I remember having a warm feeling because it was so feminine. I remember thinking you should probably plant some." This is how he thinks. Men wrote the dictionary. They are literal. Men usually say what they mean and mean what they say. The trouble arises when they expect women to do the same.

Even though women value endless layers of subtleties in what they say, when it involves a man, it's best to just literally believe him. Unless he's trying to fool you, everything he says, he means. Take him at face value.

In football, players have no trouble believing their coach. One reason is the coach is literal; he says what he means. The other reason is because in most cases the coach used to be a player. Having been a player buys the coach credibility with his players. They know he's speaking from a position of experience, from having "been there, done that." That's all they need to know.

VALUABLE LESSON	
#49	When a man speaks, he is imparting information. When he listens, he expects to receive information. Women often talk in order to process their thoughts and feelings.

This even applies to the guys in the booth calling the game. The best play-by-play announcers and color commentators are usually ex-players. My favorites were Pat Summerall and John Madden. Fans listening to their broadcast appreciated Summerall and Madden. They knew the game from the perspective of having been on the field and played. Madden had the added advantage of being a Super Bowl-winning coach. Bonus!

Men Talk/Women Talk

So, when a man speaks, he is imparting information. When he listens, he expects to receive information. That's the male rule for talking: exchanging facts, ideas, and information.

Women often talk in order to process their thoughts and feelings. Men don't get this. They're not wired that way. They listen to a woman go on about several subjects and ask, "What are you talking about?" She is using talk as a way to understand something more deeply. It's kind of "thinking out loud," and it's a perfectly valid way to process knowledge for a woman. Just don't be disappointed with men's blank glassy expressions when you express yourself this way. They don't mean anything insulting by it. Go on about your business and they'll be fine.

But if you actually want action from a man, be direct. This doesn't mean you have to be unpleasant. Just don't waste a lot of words getting to the meat and potatoes of what you want him to do. Just say it. Tell him. He'll love you for it. It's actually romantic for him.

Romantic?

Yes. And here's why…

For women, romance is: "He read my mind. He knew what I wanted before I asked for it." Do you know what that is for men? Hard, energy-draining, hit-or-miss WORK. It's not fun. And he hates it. Because there's a good chance he'll get it wrong. And men hate being wrong.

For men, romance is: a woman tells him exactly what she wants. Maybe even where he can find it. She tells him when she wants it. Now he goes out and gets it for her. He returns victorious. He presents it to her. She gushes her thanks, rewarding his successful quest profusely. The "rewarding profusely" is romance for a man.

Go ahead. Be direct. To them, "I love flowers" means "I love flowers." They don't search for hidden meanings or a implied subtext. They listen literally. They're like football. Basic. Obvious. Not subtle. No more hints, Ladies!

CHAPTER  30

WHO'S YOUR TEAM?

"Having a guy friend is a great thing for a girl... to relax with a boy and get to know him without romance."
  –From the American Girl series, A Smart Girl's Guide to Boys, by Nancy Holyoke

At the Sports Bar

Here's a small contrast that makes a big difference between men and women...

There I am at my local sports bar, drinking a glass of research for this book. I am flanked by guy fans perched on the surrounding stools. As the football game gets underway, I make several appropriate comments. They do not go unnoticed.

One of the stool guys turns to me and says, "You really know your football."

"I do," I answer. "I love this game!" So far so good.

Now comes the inevitable moment of reckoning. Stool Guy asks, "Who's your team?"

I feel all the male heads slowly turn toward me expectantly, awaiting the answer they all must have.

"Well," I say, "I was born in Chicago, so my family thinks I'm a Bears fan. But my boyfriend for many years was a Niners fanatic, so I really love them. But now I live in L.A. and since the Chargers are our closest team, and I drive down there to see the games, I guess they're my favorite team right now."

I look up. All the men's eyes have glazed over and they are looking at me as though I just beamed down from the Mother Ship. They do not initiate any further interaction with me for the rest of the quarter. It was then that I realized my mistake and the difference between men and women with respect to team loyalty.

The mistake was: I went on too long.

The difference is: men stick with their team FOREVER. No matter who they marry, no matter where they live. Win. Lose. Playoffs. Coaching changes. Player changes. Ownership changes. None of it dents a man's loyalty. He may even grumble and gripe about his team. But it's still *his* team!

Male Loyalty

Women like to be loyal to their community. Born in Indiana. Went to college in Denver. Lives in Atlanta. That's a triple combo fan of Colts-Broncos-Falcons.

Women tell me there's another reason they're reluctant to have a favorite team. It goes something like this, "Because every time I tune in to watch, my team starts losing!"

Men don't regard that as a valid reason to change loyalties. They are very serious about their team, and often quite emotional.

Case in point: My sister and her husband lived in Denver for many years. They raised their three sons there. Naturally, as you would expect, the boys, like their dad, are rabid and forever Broncos fans.

One Sunday, during a game, my sister was upstairs in one of the bedrooms, changing the sheets. She sees her eldest son, four-year-old Adam, coming into the room, shaking his little head, his lower lip trembling, tears in his eyes.

"What's the matter, honey?" she asked.

In a trembling voice, he said, "Daddy's really mad at John Elway."

My sister couldn't help laughing. She explained the difference between "real-life mad" and "football mad." "Football mad" is a manifestation of die-hard loyalty. This difference accounts for why it's important for a man to ask: Who's Your Team?

A View from the 20's

My niece, Tanya, writes an entertaining blog. Let's see what a girl in her mid 20's has to say about sports bars:

> Sports Bars are FUN! The energy and testosterone make it worth getting out of your pj's and slapping on some lip gloss. The guys are pumped, and you have great odds (the ratio of girls to guys alone is totally in our favor). Here are some Do's and Don'ts:

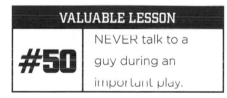

VALUABLE LESSON

#50 NEVER talk to a guy during an important play.

Do:

> • Look nice, cute and sporty: jeans, Converse sneakers, maybe even a jersey if you're feeling creative.
>
> • Order sportsy food like beer and wings. Caution: be careful, go slowly. You do NOT want to get tanked. Being "that girl" is never a good thing. Also, stay sportsy. You can have a couple of beers and look like a girl who is into sports and fun and easygoing, or you can be a girly girl

with a mai tai and an umbrella in your drink (translation: high maintenance).

• Actually look interested in the game. An occasional holler or "yeah" or "good call," or a "WOO," are all acceptable sounds to make at a bar. CAUTION: know what you're talking about before fully committing. Results could turn disastrous if you are not knowledgeable of the game or team or even the sport in general. This does not seem too hard, but you would be surprised... my girlfriend leaned over to me (when we were in front of a table of really hot guys) and whispered, "Oh good, it's the last period... ya know, the 3rd period." And yes, that would have been fine if we were watching HOCKEY!!! But in football there are QUARTERS, so yeah, we have 4 quarters. Like a DOLLAR! It's easy. Ahh, bless her heart :)

• There is only one "don't" at sports bars: NEVER talk to a guy during an important play.

CHAPTER 31

ZONE VS MAN-TO-MAN: SHOPPING VS BUYING

"Men go buying; women go shoooopping."
–Mimi Donaldson

Here's an instance where we're going to use the Defense as our best example. Whether we're talking business life or personal life, women use the *Zone Defense*, while men usually stay with *Man-To-Man*.

In football, here are the basic differences:

In a man-to-man defense, each defending player guards a corresponding player on the other team. Each player is assigned someone to "cover," shadowing him wherever he goes, blocking him, knocking down any passes thrown to him. One-on-one, man-to-man.

In a zone defense, each defensive player is given an area of the field to cover, rather than a person. Any opposing player coming into that area or "zone" is his responsibility.

Now, back to my point: Women tend to take in a number of impressions simultaneously and later focus on specifics (zone). Men on the other hand, usually start by focusing on specific facts, then move outward to encompass the big picture (man-to-man). The result is that the sexes often drive each other crazy, with men complaining that "women are not focused," while women moan that "men are not flex-ible." Both of these defensive schemes are valid approaches to life. But they are distinctly different. This difference needs to be recognized and each style needs to be appreciated.

These differences explain why women shop and men buy. Women want to take in the whole picture before zooming in on their specific goals. Men want to zoom in on their specific goals, hoping all the while they never need to take in the whole picture.

Unfortunate Example: True Story

Married couple. The wife knows the husband does not like to roam aimlessly around a store, surveying the new fashions and other merchandise, in hopes of finding something to buy. This is called "shopping," and most husbands dislike it.

> Women tend to take in a number of impressions simultaneously and later focus on specifics. Men on the other hand, usually start by focusing on specific facts, then move outward to encompass the big picture.

So, this wife says, "Oh, please take me shopping, honey. I just want to buy one pair of shoes, and I know right where they are."

"Okay," he answers, envisioning a relatively short trip, since she wants to buy "one pair of shoes," and she knows "right where they are."

Besides, he needs the points; they had been fighting a lot. He sees a way to cut his losses and maybe score a touchdown. He dutifully allots two hours of energy to the trip. In his mind he will be home by 4:00.

They get to the mall. He finds a parking place right away. In his mind, he is ahead of schedule. This makes him happy. His puts his arm around her. As they enter the store, he sees the shoe department. As he turns to tell her it's over to the right, he sees her start to wander the opposite way, to the left.

"Honey," he says, pointing to the right. "The shoes are over there."

"I know, I know," she says, with a hint of a dismissive tone. "I just have to look."

He starts doing a slow burn. "She said shoes. I distinctly remember her saying shoes." He thought she'd go right to the shoes. He can feel two hours of energy start draining out.

The slow burn slowly picks up more steam. She just said, "I

> That's why stores have those little chairs outside the dressing room — for men whose women have lied to them and tricked them into "shopping."

have to look." He involuntarily consults his internal dictionary, looking up the definition of "has to." It means "obligated to, has a duty to." He knows she doesn't *have* to look; she WANTS to look. More energy drains out. He needs to rest.

That's why stores have those little chairs outside the dressing room — for men whose women have lied to them and tricked them into "shopping."

And it isn't over yet.

With her laser shopping vision, she spies the perfect blouse with the kind of collar she's been searching for.

Pop Quiz

Did she...

A) Make a mental note of the blouse, go to the shoe department, buy the shoes, take him home, and come back for the blouse later?

Or...

B) Say "Oh, honey, I just have to stop and try on this blouse," making him wait and completely depleting what little energy he had left?

HINT: He told his divorce lawyer, "That was the final straw. She lied to me for the last time."

She told her divorce lawyer, "That's his *problem*. He's not *flexible* enough. He doesn't *flow* with it."

Not a pretty ending, but an ending that must be told, in the hope that it prevents similar endings.

VALUABLE LESSON	
#51	It's always best to choose, before the game starts, which direction a two-gender excursion will take.

Men's disdain for shopping starts early. My friend's little boy used to love shopping with Mommy. Then one day, out of the blue, when he was about four years old, he stopped in the middle of the mall, stomped his little cowboy boot on the floor and said, tearfully, "Mom, do you know where we're going? Or are we just gonna wander around?"

This little boy was only four! And already he knows: women shop and men buy.

My advice: If the two of you simply MUST go to the mall together, decide if you're going with the zone or the man-to-man approach. That way, both parties can agree in advance and there aren't any surprises. It's always best to choose, before the game starts, which direction a two-gender excursion will take.

CHAPTER  32

A PARTING SHOT: HOW FOOTBALL SAVED MY LIFE

"In the course of the game, there's always that adversity you
will face. Stay even keel, poised and confident, and know that
if you continue to fight, good things will happen."
 –Drew Brees, MVP, Super Bowl 2009

Tackling My Disease

It was the start of the football season in 2006. I had been messing around with a potentially life threatening disease for over two years. "Messing around" means I had tried various treatments that had not quite finished the job. The disease was not quite obliterated. I could not afford to ignore it; it was not that kind of thing. Previously, I had experienced pulled muscles from physical workouts and an eye cornea condition, small things that healed themselves with rest or a little medicine. This was my first serious health issue. So I tackled this disease as a fight for victory — just like on the football field. Drew Brees said it well in the quote above, when he visited a little boy in the hospital.

My doctor advised me it was time for the big guns. This involved several extended hospital stays, each stay two weeks or more. Each part of the treatment took more time than originally planned. (See Murphy's

Law: Everything takes longer than you think.) I always say you teach what you most need to learn. I actually keep forgetting Murphy's Law, and patience is one of my life lessons.

So it was September, 2006. Nine months earlier I had made plans to go to the NFL Pro Bowl — the all-star game of football — in Honolulu in early 2007. I had bought airline tickets for me and my much beloved football fan nephew. My fabulous travel agent, Roxana Lewis had found us a wonderful hotel for a great price. I told the doctors I would endure all the treatments, but that I was leaving February 8th for Hawaii. Doctors don't like dates dictated to them, and they wouldn't guarantee anything. But they did say it may be possible.

Teaching the Nurses

Then, since Murphy's Law is a "law," the September treatment dragged into October. I found myself in the hospital watching football on Saturdays (college) and Sundays and Monday nights (NFL). Nurses would come in, look at the TV and sniff disparagingly. "You're watching football?" they would ask, a bit incredulous.

VALUABLE LESSON
#52 Anything is possible when human beings are committed and passionate and determined to fight.

"Yes," I would answer. "It's fabulous."

"Really?" they would say, with doubt in their tone. "That's why I'm working weekends; my husband is glued to the games." And they would all roll their eyes and do the "tsk-sigh" thing.

"No, really," I said. "You say I have such a positive attitude. Well, watching this game motivates me to think anything is possible when human beings are committed and passionate and determined to fight. That's what you teach your patients. That's the reason I'm inspired to fight this disease and win." Then I would quote Coach Herm Edwards,

"You play to win the game." My passion for the game and winning may save my life, I would tell them.

I got through to most of them, and they would stay in my room awhile. I taught them the basics of watching football and how to enjoy it. Yes, I pointed out the great thighs and the dramatic plays — all of it now in Chapter 3 of this book.

Playoffs: Life Saving

By the time the playoffs came around, my San Diego Chargers fuzzy throw blanket was on my hospital bed, and groups of nurses were gathering for lessons. Some told me that my lessons enabled them to enjoy the game with their husbands or boyfriends. I may have even saved a marriage or two.

The treatment and hospital stays got more intense. In December, when my friend visited, I was on morphine and was a bit out of it. I said, "I have to watch the playoffs." She said my only coherent statements were when I pointed out inspiring plays on the football field. She later said, "Football saved you, Mimi." I was stunned; I had not thought of that before. Now I realize football not only helped save my life. The time in the hospital teaching the nurses how to watch football was the inspiration for this book.

VALUABLE LESSON

#53 An effective way to reach your goals: put them in writing, and get the people around you aligned with them.

I was determined to make the Pro Bowl in Hawaii. So when the December stay reached into January, I put "February 8th to Hawaii" up on the bulletin board in my room, and got all the nurses and doctors enrolled in my goal. This is always an effective way to reach your goals: put them in writing, and get the people around you aligned with them.

My blood stats had to be at a certain place for me to get out of the hospital. So the numbers went up on the board and became more goals — just like points on the field.

And I did it! I got released on January 26th. TOUCHDOWN! I was weak, but my doctor assured me "people can recover in Hawaii."

I did not disappoint myself or my nephew. We had a great time. I will let him finish the story.

Mark's Story

Ever since I can remember, my two older brothers and I have experienced "Camp Mimi," a dreamy individual week vacation with our beloved aunt and your very own author. Living in chilly Connecticut, I loved trading the snow for the sun and coming out to her waterfront place to eat breakfast in bed, watch scary movies, and stay up late. "Camp Mimi" is always extravagant, always adventurous. Yet, in early 2006, when Mimi insisted on taking me to the Pro Bowl in early 2007, I was truly blown away. You have to understand that my parents aren't quite as keen on NFL football as my aunt and I am (my mom pulled me out of pee wee football in second grade after a broken finger). So when Mimi called telling me that she would be taking me to an NFL game, an NFL game in Hawaii, an NFL Pro Bowl game, and that we'd be sitting on the 50-yard line, I busted out in what fans might call a Lambeau Leap-type celebration. The date was set to leave February 8th, and I could hardly wait.

It was around the time football season started when my mom began sacking my excitement every time

I brought the Pro Bowl up. "It may not happen, Mark," she would say. "Don't get your hopes up." But breaking a promise with me is like telling Terrell Owens he's not the best wide receiver in the game. It just doesn't happen. So as the Sundays passed and the playoffs became imminent, my anticipation mounted. I fantasized watching the best players in the game under a sun-drenched sky with my favorite aunt. I wasn't aware of the details of her medical condition, and even if I had been, I know that if anyone can defy the odds, it's Mimi. Her enthusiasm for the game meshed with mine, and we both didn't hope, but knew, we would make it to Hawaii.

Mimi was released from the hospital just two weeks before we left for Hawaii, right in time for the Super Bowl. Mimi plans her schedule not according to the normal calendar, but the Football Calendar. Don't call her on the day of rest! We left on a Thursday—a school day. I remember this distinctly because all my friends were jealous that I was going.

We spent Friday seeing some sights and visiting the beach. While most newly-released hospital patients are curled up in their beds, Mimi was fiercely leading me through a gorgeous Honolulu. By leading, I mean she was the one getting up first, persuading me to walk instead of take a taxi, and most of all, inspiring me with her zeal and optimism. It was a sight to behold. We went to sleep that night giggling about what we'd been looking forward to for over a year.

The day of the Pro Bowl arrived, and Mimi and I made our way to Aloha Stadium. We arrived in our 50-yard-line seats, just as promised. We watched a surprisingly competitive game between the AFC and NFC, and cheered as San Diego Chargers' kicker, Nate Kaeding, punched a final-second field goal through the uprights to win the game. Our family loves Nate: he went to University of Iowa, which is Mimi's alma mater as well as my mom and dad's. It exceeded every expectation imaginable, and is a day that I'll remember for the rest of my life.

On the way home we were sitting in the Honolulu airport, reminiscing about all the inspiring plays we witnessed and how some of our favorite players had performed. All of a sudden, I heard someone behind me whisper, "Is that Drew Brees?" I looked to where he was pointing. Seeing a built guy, a beautiful wife, and an unmistakable birthmark, I realized that one of the best QB's in the league was sitting only a short pass away. Mimi kept her cool as I proceeded to freak out. She handed me a piece of paper she had in her purse and said only two words: "Do it." So I got up, walked over, met a now Super Bowl MVP, and returned with an autograph. It was the game-winning field goal to a touchdown of a trip.

Mimi's Coda

I beat the odds. I played to win. I attended the Pro Bowl. I was only a spectator, but being in the stadium, watching the best of the best NFL players, with my nephew at my side, I knew I was in great company. I had just fought the biggest fight of my life to get to the Pro Bowl, just as the players on the field had fought to get there. The players came to win that day, but I knew I had already won.